BPP UNIVERSITY

D1387176

B

21ST CENTURY COMMUNICATION
LISTENING, SPEAKING, AND CRITICAL THINKING

1

LIDA BAKER

LAURIE BLASS

BPP University

107117

Australia • Brazil • Mexico • Singapore • United Kingdom • United States

NATIONAL GEOGRAPHIC LEARNING | **CENGAGE Learning®**

21st Century Communication: Listening, Speaking, and Critical Thinking
Student Book 1
Lida Baker and Laurie Blass

Publisher: Sherrise Roehr

Executive Editor: Laura Le Dréan

Managing Editor: Jennifer Monaghan

Senior Development Editor: Mary Whittemore

Associate Development Editor: Lisl Trowbridge

Media Research: Leila Hishmeh

Executive Marketing Manager: Ben Rivera

Product Marketing Manager: Anders Bylund

Sr. Director, Production: Michael Burggren

Manager, Production: Daisy Sosa

Content Project Manager: Mark Rzeszutek

Manufacturing Planner: Mary Beth Hennebury

Interior Design: Brenda Carmichael

Compositor: SPi Global

© 2017 National Geographic Learning, a part of Cengage Learning

ALL RIGHTS RESERVED. No part of this work covered by the copyright herein may be reproduced or distributed in any form or by any means, except as permitted by U.S. copyright law, without the prior written permission of the copyright owner.

"National Geographic", "National Geographic Society" and the Yellow Border Design are registered trademarks of the National Geographic Society
® Marcas Registradas

For product information and technology assistance, contact us at
Cengage Learning Customer & Sales Support, cengage.com/contact

For permission to use material from this text or product, submit all requests online at **cengage.com/permissions**
Further permissions questions can be emailed to
permissionrequest@cengage.com

Student Book:
ISBN: 978-1-305-94592-0

Student Book with Online Workbook Sticker Code:
ISBN: 978-1-33-727580-4

National Geographic Learning
20 Channel Center Street
Boston, MA 02210
USA

National Geographic Learning, a Cengage Learning Company, has a mission to bring the world to the classroom and the classroom to life. With our English language programs, students learn about their world by experiencing it. Through our partnerships with National Geographic and TED, they develop the language and skills they need to be successful global citizens and leaders.

Locate your local office at **international.cengage.com/region**

Visit National Geographic Learning online at **NGL.cengage.com**
Visit our corporate website at **www.cengage.com**

Printed in the United States of America
Print Number: 01 Print Year: 2016

Reviewers

The authors and publisher would like to thank the following teachers from all over the world for their valuable input during the development process of the 21st Century Communication series.

BPP UNIVERSITY
LIBRARY AND
INFORMATION SERVICES

Coleeta P. Abdullah, *EducationKSA, Saudi Arabia*

Ghada Al Attar, *AMIDEAST, Yemen*

Yazeed Al Jeddawy, *AMIDEAST, United Kingdom*

Zubidah Al Sallami, *AMIDEAST, Netherlands*

Ammar Al-Hawi, *AMIDEAST, Yemen*

William Albertson, *Drexel University English Language Center, Pennsylvania*

Tara Arntsen, *Northern State University, South Dakota*

Kevin Ballou, *Kobe College, Japan*

Nafisa Bintayeh, *AMIDEAST, Yemen*

Linda Bolet, *Houston Community College, Texas*

Tony Carnerie, *UCSD Extension, English Language Institute, California*

Catherine Cheetham, *Tokai University, Japan*

Celeste Coleman, *CSUSM American Language and Culture Institute, California*

Amy Cook, *Bowling Green State University, Ohio*

Katie Cottier, *University of Texas at Austin, Texas*

Teresita Curbelo, *Instituto Cultural Anglo Uruguayo, Uruguay*

Sarah de Pina, *ELS Boston Downtown, Massachusetts*

Rachel DeSanto, *Hillsborough Community College, Florida*

Silvana Dushku, *Intensive English Institute, Illinois*

Jennie Farnell, *University of Bridgeport, Connecticut*

Rachel Fernandez, *UCI Extension, International Programs, California*

Alayne Flores, *UCSD Extension, English Language Institute, California*

Claire Gimble, *Virginia International University, Virginia*

Floyd H. Graham III, *Kansai Gaidai University, Japan*

Kuei-ping Hsu, *National Tsing Hua University, Taiwan*

James Hughes, *Massachusetts International Academy / UMass Boston, Massachusetts*

Mariano Ignacio, *Centro Universitario de Idiomas, Argentina*

Jules L. Janse van Rensburg, *Chinese Culture University, South Africa*

Rachel Kadish, *GEOS Languages Plus Boston, Massachusetts*

Anthony Lavigne, *Kansai Gaidai University, Japan*

Ai-ping Liu, *National Central University Language Center, Taiwan*

Debra Liu, *City College of San Francisco, California*

Wilder Yesid Escobar Almeciga Imeciga, *Universidad El Bosque, Colombia*

Christina Lorimer, *SDSU American Language Institute, California*

Joanna Luper, *Liberty University, Virginia*

Joy MacFarland, *FLS Boston Commons, Massachusetts*

Elizabeth Mariscal, *UCSD Extension, English Language Institute, California*

Susan McAlister, *Language & Culture Center, University of Houston, Texas*

Wendy McBride, *Spring International Language Center at the University of Arkansas, Arkansas*

Monica McCrory, *University of Texas, Texas*

Katy Montgomery, *Purdue University, Indiana*

Katherine Murphy, *Massachusetts International Academy, Massachusetts*

Emily Naber, *Washington English Center, Washington*

Kavitha Nambisan, *University of Tennessee-Martin, Tennessee*

Sandra Navarro, *Glendale Community College, California*

Fernanda Ortiz, *Center for English as a Second Language at the University of Arizona, Arizona*

Pamela Patterson, *Seminole State College, Oklahoma*

Grace Pimcias, *CSUSM American Language and Culture Institute, California*

Jennie Popp, *Universidad Andres Bello, Chile*

Jamie Reinstein, *Community College of Philadelphia, Pennsylvania*

Philip Rice, *University of Delaware, Delaware*

Helen Roland, *Miami Dade College, Florida*

Yoko Sakurai, *Aichi University, Japan*

Jenay Seymour, *Hongik University (Sejong Campus), South Korea*

Margaret Shippey, *Miami Dade College, Florida*

William Slade, *University of Texas at Austin, Texas*

Kelly Smith, *UCSD Extension, English Language Institute, California*

Rachel Stokes, *University of Texas at Austin, Texas*

Joshua Stone, *Approach International Student Center, Massachusetts*

Judy Tanka, *UCLA Extension, California*

Mary M. Wang, *University of Wisconsin-Madison, Wisconsin*

Judy Wong, *Pace University, New York*

Scope and Sequence

PRONUNCIATION SKILL	NOTE-TAKING SKILL	TED TALKS	PRESENTATION SKILL	UNIT ASSIGNMENT
Syllable stress	Use an outline	*How to use a paper towel* **Joe Smith**	Focus your topic	Give a group presentation on tips to help the environment
Thought groups and pausing	Use abbreviations and symbols	*Photos from a storm chaser* **Camille Seaman**	Use visual aids	Give an individual presentation describing a time when you felt connected to nature
Statement intonation	Indent details	*A skateboard with a boost* **Sanjay Dastoor**	Rehearse your presentation	Participate in a panel discussion about ecofriendly methods of transportation
Contractions with *be*	Write key words or short sentences	*Why I take the piano on the road ... and in the air* **Daria van den Bercken**	Use an effective hook	Give an individual presentation describing your music-listening style
Sentence stress	Use a mind map	*Why lunch ladies are heroes* **Jarrett J. Krosoczka**	Tell a personal story	Give an individual presentation describing an experience of giving or receiving thanks
Intonation in questions	Use a T-chart	*3 rules to spark learning* **Ramsey Musallam**	Consider your audience	Give an individual presentation about a time when your curiosity led you to learn or try something new
Linking	Review your notes	*How to reinvent the apartment building* **Moshe Safdie**	Organize a problem-solution presentation	Give an individual presentation describing a building or public space that makes a city or town more livable
Vowels in unstressed syllables	Record definitions	*3 things I learned while my plane crashed* **Ric Elias**	Have a strong conclusion	Give an individual presentation about a change you made or want to make

Welcome to 21st Century Communication

21st Century Communication: Listening, Speaking, and Critical Thinking develops essential listening, speaking, and presentation skills to help learners succeed with their academic and professional goals. Students learn key academic skills as they engage with thought-provoking TED Talks and 21st century themes and skills such as global awareness, information literacy, and critical thinking.

Each unit opens with an impactful photograph related to a **21st century theme** and Think and Discuss questions to draw students into the topic.

Part 1 introduces a variety of **listening inputs** including lectures, interviews, podcasts, and classroom discussions. Selected listenings are accompanied by video slide shows.

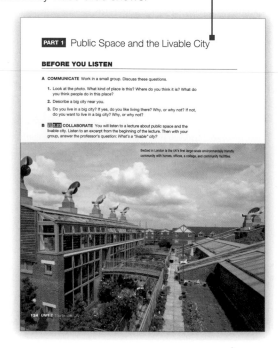

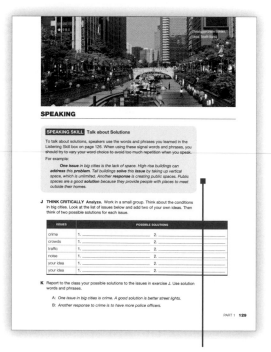

Llistening, speaking, note-taking, and pronunciation skills are explicitly taught and practiced. Woven throughout are 21st century skills of **collaboration, communication,** and **critical thinking.**

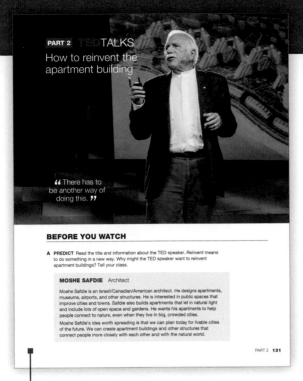

PART 2 TEDTALKS
How to reinvent the
apartment building

*" There has to
be another way of
doing this. "*

BEFORE YOU WATCH

A PREDICT Read the title and information about the TED speaker. *Reinvent* means
to do something in a new way. Why might the TED speaker want to reinvent
apartment buildings? Tell your class.

MOSHE SAFDIE Architect

Moshe Safdie is an Israeli/Canadian/American architect. He designs apartments,
museums, airports, and other structures. He is interested in public spaces that
improve cities and towns. Safdie also builds apartments that let in natural light
and include lots of open space and gardens. He wants his apartments to help
people connect to nature, even when they live in big, crowded cities.

Moshe Safdie's idea worth spreading is that we can plan today for livable cities
of the future. We can create apartment buildings and other structures that
connect people more closely with each other and with the natural world.

PART 2 **131**

Part 2 introduces the TED speaker and the idea
worth spreading. Students explore and discuss
the ideas while at the same time seamlessly
applying the skills learned in Part 1.

Infographics engage students more
deeply with the unit theme and promote
visual literacy.

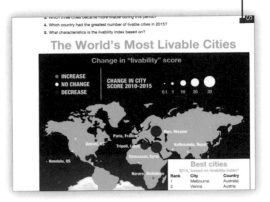

The World's Most Livable Cities

Change in "livability" score

Presentation Skills
inspired by the TED
speakers give students
the skills and authentic
language they need
to successfully
deliver their own
presentations.

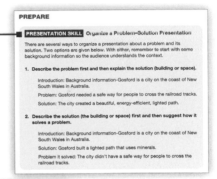

PREPARE

PRESENTATION SKILL Organize a Problem-Solution Presentation

There are several ways to organize a presentation about a problem and its
solution. Two options are given below. With either, remember to start with some
background information so the audience understands the context.

1. Describe the problem first and then explain the solution (building or space).

    Introduction: Background information-Gosford is a city on the coast of New
    South Wales in Australia.

    Problem: Gosford needed a safe way for people to cross the railroad tracks.

    Solution: The city created a beautiful, energy-efficient, lighted path.

2. Describe the solution (the building or space) first and then suggest how it
    solves a problem.

    Introduction: Background information-Gosford is a city on the coast of New
    South Wales in Australia.

    Solution: Gosford built a lighted path that uses minerals.

    Problem it solved: The city didn't have a safe way for people to cross the
    railroad tracks.

Put It Together helps students **connect
ideas** and prepares them for their
final assignment. Students synthesize
information and consolidate their learning.

REFLECT

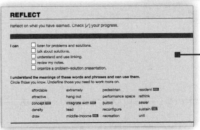

Reflect encourages
students to **take
charge of their
learning**, another
21st century skill.

Put It Together

A THINK CRITICALLY Synthesize. Work in a small group. Answer these questions.
Use examples from the lecture in Part 1 and the TED Talk in Part 2 in your
discussion.

1. What did planners do to make cities more livable?

2. In your opinion, which of the planners' ideas is the most useful or important? Why?

B THINK CRITICALLY Analyze. Are there any public spaces, buildings, or other
projects in your area that are similar to the ones in the Part 1 lecture or the TED
Talk? If yes, list them. Explain how they draw people together, increase safety, help
people connect with nature, or make your area more livable in some way. If no,
propose a space, building, or other project that your community should consider.

COMMUNICATE

ASSIGNMENT: Give an Individual Presentation You will give an individual
presentation about a building or public space that makes a city or town more
livable. Explain how this building or space solves a problem of city living.

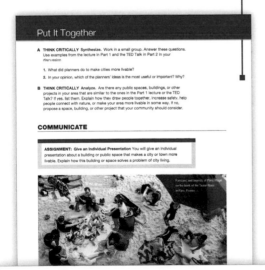

COMMUNICATE

ASSIGNMENT: Give an Individual Presentation You will give an individual
presentation about a building or public space that makes a city or town more
livable. Explain how this building or space solves a problem of city living.

Unit 2, Part 2 **Watch**

INSTRUCTIONS

Watch the video. Drag the correct words to complete the sentences. There are two extra words. Then click **Submit** to check your answers.

| touch | daughter | perspire | photographs |
| atmosphere | monsters | super cell | grandfather |

1. We can infer that Camille Seaman's _____ was an inspiration to her.

2. Camille's _____ encouraged her to begin storm chasing.

3. The _____ is a type of giant cloud.

4. When Camille says that storm chasing is "a very tactile experience," she means that she feels like she can _____ the clouds.

Fully blended **Online Workbooks powered by
MyELT** help develop **digital literacy skills** by
offering students the complete audio and video
program along with speech-recognition and auto-
graded language practice activities.

ix

Small Actions, Big Results

Jadav Payeng began planting trees on the island of Majuli in India in 1979 to keep the island from getting smaller. He has planted thousands of plants, which have become the 1,360-acre Molai Forest. The forest has saved the island and has become a habitat for several endangered species, including elephants and Bengal tigers.

THINK AND DISCUSS

1 Read the unit title. What do you think it means?

2 Describe the photo. What do you see?

3 Read the caption. How does Jadav's story relate to the title? Explain.

BEFORE YOU LISTEN

A COMMUNICATE Work in small groups. Discuss these questions.

1. Look at the photo. What is the man doing? Why?

2. What kinds of water problems do people have in different parts of the world?

3. Do you feel a responsibility to change the way you use water? Why, or why not? If yes, in what way?

B THINK CRITICALLY Predict. You are going to hear a TV interview. The guest speaker will give tips (suggestions) for saving water. Will this information be important for you? Why, or why not? Discuss your ideas with your group.

Joe Del Bosque picks a piece of asparagus at the Del Bosque Inc. farm in Firebaugh, California, USA.

VOCABULARY

c 🎧 **1.2** Read and listen to the sentences with words from the TV interview. Guess the meaning of each bold word or phrase. Then write each word or phrase next to its definition.

a. Australia is very rich in natural **resources**, including coal, copper, iron, gold, and uranium.

b. One way to **conserve** electricity is to turn off the lights when you leave a room.

c. Each month, the government publishes **statistics** about the number of people who found and lost jobs.

d. You shouldn't use the dishwasher when it is only half full because it **wastes** water.

e. I probably drink eight glasses of water a day **on average**; some days I drink more and some days less.

f. When I moved to an apartment near my job, I **cut** my driving time from 30 minutes to 10 minutes.

g. Lake Ontario is **huge**. It looks like an ocean!

h. The professor **requires** students to turn off their cell phones in his class.

i. There's water on the bathroom floor. I think the bathtub has a **leak**.

j. It's **crucial** to drink water after you exercise. Your body needs it.

1. _____crucial_____ (adj) extremely important

2. _____ (n) natural or man-made products that people need or can use

3. _____ (adj) very, very large

4. _____ (adv) usually, normally

5. _____ (v) save

6. _____ (v) makes it necessary for someone to do something

7. _____ (v) use less of something or make something smaller

8. _____ (n) a hole or opening that allows water or gas to escape

9. _____ (v) uses too much of something, or uses it in a bad way

10. _____ (n) numbers that give information

D COMMUNICATE Work with a partner. Take turns asking and answering the questions. Use the words in bold in your answers.

> A: *How long does it take you to get to work or school, **on average?***
>
> B: ***On average,** it takes about 20-25 minutes. It depends on the traffic.*

1. How long does it take you to get to work or school, **on average?**

2. When you were younger, what is something your parents **required** you to do? What are some things your teacher **requires** you to do for this class?

3. Finish this sentence:
   For me to be healthy, it is **crucial** to _____ every day.

4. Do you ever **waste** money? If yes, how?

5. How can people **cut** the amount of time they spend online?

6. If you receive a **huge** amount of food in a restaurant, do you eat it all? If not, what do you do with the food you don't finish?

7. Do you try to **conserve** water? How?

LISTEN

E 🎧 **1.3** ▶ **1.1** **LISTEN FOR MAIN IDEAS** Read the statements. Then listen to the TV interview. Choose the answer that best completes each statement.

1. The interview is mainly about _____.
   a. World Water Day
   b. reducing your water bill
   c. simple ways to save water

2. According to Chandra Cassidy, it is important for everyone to save water because _____. (Choose the two correct answers.)
   a. the world's climate is changing
   b. people can save money on their water bills
   c. there isn't enough fresh water
   d. many poor people don't have any water

3. Cassidy's main message is that _____.
   a. most people are paying too much for water
   b. we can help the environment by changing our behavior in small ways
   c. the world's population is growing too fast

LISTENING SKILL Listen for Numbers and Statistics

Listening for numbers and statistics can help you understand how the speaker supports the main ideas.

Main idea: *Worldwide, people are using and wasting huge amounts of plastic.*

Supporting statistics: *For example, Americans throw away 35 million plastic bottles a year. Americans throw away about 91 percent of the plastic they use.*

F 🎧 **1.4** **LISTEN FOR DETAILS** Listen to segments from the TV interview. Write the missing numbers.

Segment 1

1. Water covers _____ percent of the earth, but less than _____ percent is fresh water.

2. Right now we have almost _____ people on earth.

3. In 30 years the population is going to be _____.

Segment 2

4. It takes _____ gallons of water to produce just one pound of beef.

5. Leaks can waste more than _____ gallons a year. That's more than _____ percent of all the water we use.

Woman drawing water from a well in Thar Desert, Rajasthan, India

NOTE-TAKING SKILL Use an Outline

One way to remember the things you hear is to make an outline of the speaker's most important ideas. A simple outline looks like this:

I. Saving Water

   A. Why is it crucial to save water?

      1. Save money

      2. Not enough fresh water in the world

(See page 170 in the *Independent Student Handbook* for more information on using outlines.)

G 🎧 **1.5** Listen to segment 3 of the interview. Complete the outline.

   I. Saving Water

     A. Why is it crucial to save water?

        1. Save money

        2. Not enough fresh water in the world

     B. Tips for saving water at home

        1. Don't run the _____ water _____ when you _____

        2. Take _____

        3. Don't eat _____

        4. Fix _____

AFTER YOU LISTEN

H COMMUNICATE Work in a group. Use your answers to exercises E, F, and G to discuss the questions.

1. The program host, Harry Martinez, says it's important for "*everyone*—not just people in dry places—to save water." Why is it important for people in areas with enough water to think about conserving it?

2. Review the reasons we need to save water from exercise E, item 2. Which reason is more important for you? Why? Can you think of other reasons?

3. Look at the outline in exercise G. Do you follow any of these tips now? If so, which ones? Do you think you might try to follow them in the future? Which tip is or will be the most difficult for you to follow? Why?

Where does our water go?

The average U.S. household uses 265 gallons of water each day.

Here's how it's used . . .

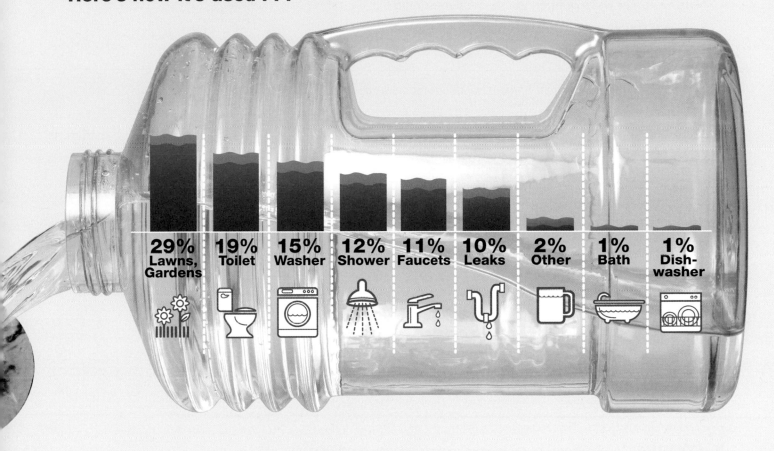

29% Lawns, Gardens 19% Toilet 15% Washer 12% Shower 11% Faucets 10% Leaks 2% Other 1% Bath 1% Dish-washer

1. How many gallons does the average American family use each day?

2. What percentage of their water do Americans use outdoors?

3. Which indoor item uses the most water? Does this surprise you? Why, or why not?

4. Which water uses do you think are part of "Other"?

5. The graph gives average numbers. The percentages will be higher or lower in different places. What do you think the graph would look like in your country?

SPEAKING

SPEAKING SKILL Give Tips or Suggestions

To give tips or suggestions, we often use the *imperative* form. The imperative form does not have a subject. We understand that the subject is *you*. Imperatives begin with an affirmative or negative verb:

- **Fix** *leaky faucets.*
- **Don't eat** *meat.*

Here are other ways of offering tips or suggestions:

- *You should / shouldn't eat meat.*
- *It's (not) a good idea to take long showers.*

(See page 167 in the *Independent Student Handbook* for more information on using outlines.)

J COLLABORATE Work in a small group. Complete the outline below with tips for saving water. Use the verbs in the box or choose your own.

fix	(don't) run	(don't) take	(don't) water	(don't) flush
turn off	cut	(don't) use	replace	fill

   I. Saving Water

      A. Why is it crucial to save water?

      B. Tips for saving water at home

      C. More tips for saving water
           Replace leaky faucets

        1. _____   4. _____

        2. _____   5. _____

        3. _____   6. _____

K COMMUNICATE Share your tips from exercise J with another group.

PRONUNCIATION SKILL Syllable Stress

A syllable is a single unit of speech. Words have one or more syllables. For example, *drink* has one syllable. *Water* has two syllables. In words with two or more syllables, one of the syllables is stressed (pronounced a little louder and more clearly). Listen to these examples. The stressed syllables are in bold.

🎧 **1.6**

Two syllables: **wa**-ter   Three syllables: **nat**-u-ral   Four syllables: en-**vi**-ron-ment

(See page 172 in the *Independent Student Handbook* for more information on using outlines.)

L 🎧 **1.7** Listen to the words from the interview. Underline the stressed syllables.

| con-serv-ing | e-nough | sta-tis-tics | leak-y |
| per-cent | pop-u-la-tion | sug-ges-tions | wast-ed |

M Work with a partner. Say the words in exercise L. Stress the correct syllable.

N **COMMUNICATE** Work with a partner. Read the sentences silently. Pay attention to the bolded, stressed syllables below. Then read the sentences aloud. Guess if the sentences are true or false. Check your answers on page 21.

A: *About 50 percent of the world's fresh water is stored in **gla**ciers.*
B: *I guess that's true.*

Water Facts Quiz

		True	False
1	About 50 percent of the world's fresh water is stored in **gla**ciers.	◯	◯
2	Seventy percent of the **hu**man brain is water.	◯	◯
3	Water ex**pands** when it freezes.	◯	◯
4	It is not **pos**sible for fish to drown.	◯	◯
5	There is no **wa**ter on the moon.	◯	◯
6	It takes 10 **gal**lons of water to grow one apple.	◯	◯
7	One percent of the world's water is **drink**able.	◯	◯
8	Hot water is **heav**ier than cold water.	◯	◯
9	It takes **al**most 3,000 gallons of water to make a pair of blue jeans.	◯	◯
10	A man held his breath under**wa**ter for 30 minutes.	◯	◯

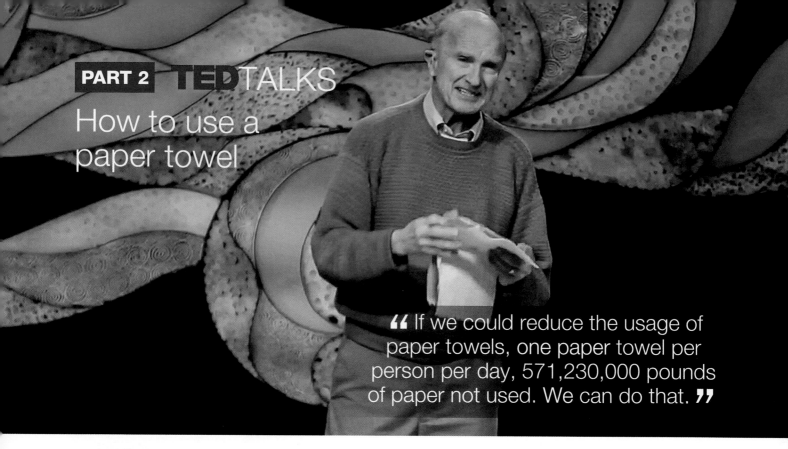

How to use a paper towel

" If we could reduce the usage of paper towels, one paper towel per person per day, 571,230,000 pounds of paper not used. We can do that. "

BEFORE YOU WATCH

A THINK CRITICALLY Predict. Read the title and the information about the TED speaker. What do you think this talk will be about? Tell your class.

> **JOE SMITH**   Lawyer and Political Activist
>
> Joe Smith is a lawyer who is also active in Oregon state and U.S. national politics. He volunteers his time to help many nonprofit organizations. In his professional life and volunteer activities, he has worked on issues he cares about to improve life for people in his community.
>
> Joe Smith's idea worth spreading is that there are very simple steps we can take to reduce our environmental impact—starting with a smarter way to use paper towels.

B COMMUNICATE Think about your answers to the following questions. Then share your answers with a partner.

> A: *I use paper towels in public restrooms.*
> B: *Me, too. I also use them in the bathroom at school.*

1. Where do you usually use paper towels?

2. On average, how many paper towels do you use to dry your hands?

3. Is there a "right" way and a "wrong" way to use a paper towel?

4. Why should we think about how we use paper towels?

VOCABULARY

C 🎧 1.8 The sentences below will help you learn words in the edited TED Talk. Read and listen to the sentences. Choose the meaning of each word in bold.

1. I used a calculator to add the long list of **figures.**
   a. names
   b. shapes
   c. numbers

2. Don't throw your paper in the trash; **recycle** it instead.
   a. organize
   b. reuse
   c. write on

3. Our gas bill is huge! We need to **reduce** the amount of energy we use each month.
   a. make larger
   b. make smaller
   c. pay back

4. When the paper towel comes out of an automatic machine, you need to **tear** it **off** before you can use it.
   a. remove
   b. save
   c. buy

5. Please take the rug outside and **shake** it to remove the dust.

    a. sell immediately

    b. move up and down or side to side

    c. throw away

6. After I do my laundry, I **fold** my clothes and put them in the drawer.

    a. wash again

    b. check before using

    c. make smaller by bending

7. I think the smartphone is the most amazing **invention** of the 21st century.

    a. new, man-made creation

    b. expensive toy

    c. type of fashion

8. I **waved** to my friend in the parking lot, but she didn't see me.

    a. moved my hand to get someone's attention

    b. shouted to get someone's attention

    c. talked to get someone's attention

9. After he washed his hands, Bob dried them with a paper towel from the **dispenser** on the wall.

    a. place where you throw something away

    b. machine that dries your hands

    c. machine that gives you something

10. The medical tests **proved** that my uncle did not have cancer.

    a. asked a question

    b. showed something

    c. hoped is true

D **COMMUNICATE** Work with a partner. Take turns asking and answering the questions with words from exercise C. Use the bold words in your answers.

> A: *Do you **recycle?** If yes, what do you recycle?*
> B: *Let's see . . . I **recycle** plastic, paper, and glass.*

1. Do you **recycle?** If yes, what do you recycle?

2. In your culture, is it usual for people to **shake** hands when they meet for the first time?

3. In your opinion, what is the most useful **invention** in the last 10 years?

4. What is easier for you to understand, words or **figures?** Give an example.

5. What is the best way to **reduce** the amount of paper we use?

6. Is there a drink **dispenser** at your school? Which drinks does it sell?

7. How can you **prove** that you are a citizen of your country?

8. Besides clothes, what else do we **fold?**

WATCH

E ▶ **1.2** **WATCH FOR MAIN IDEAS** Read the statements. Then watch the edited TED Talk and check [✓] the main idea.

1. _____ There are many kinds of paper towel dispensers.

2. _____ You should follow two steps to use a paper towel correctly.

3. _____ People waste too much paper.

4. _____ We should use recycled paper to dry our hands.

F **THINK CRITICALLY** **Reflect.** Work with a partner. Compare your answer to exercise E. Then discuss these questions.

1. Besides paper towels, what are some other kinds of paper we should try to conserve?

2. Think of your daily life. Where do you see paper waste?

3. Some restrooms do not have paper towel dispensers. What do they have instead for people to dry their hands?

learn**more** Paper towels were invented by Arthur Scott in 1907. He created them for people to use instead of cloth towels in public restrooms. He thought that using paper towels would prevent the spread of cold germs. Now, of all the paper towels used in the United States, one-third are used in public places, and two-thirds are used at home.

Man climbing a wall of recycled paper

G ▶ **1.3 WATCH FOR DETAILS** Watch segments of the edited TED Talk. Follow the directions for each part.

Segment 1 Answer the questions.

1. According to Joe Smith, how many paper towels do Americans use each year?
   a. 130 million
   b. 13 billion
   c. 30 billion

2. Joe Smith wants each person to use one less paper towel per day. If we do this, how many pounds of paper can we save in a year?
   a. 571,230,000
   b. 57,100,230
   c. 517,130,000

3. How many recycled paper towels do people normally use to dry their hands?
   a. three
   b. four
   c. five

4. What is special about the paper towel dispenser Smith describes in the building?
   a. It stops dispensing as soon as you tear.
   b. It is smarter than people.
   c. It dispenses half towels.

Segment 2 Complete the outline. Write the main idea from exercise E on the first line. Then listen and write the steps for using a paper towel correctly on the lines below.

I. _____

    A. _____

    B. _____

H THINK CRITICALLY Reflect. Work with a partner. Compare your answers to exercise G. Then discuss your answers to these questions.

1. Why does Smith start his talk with the number of paper towels that Americans use each year?

2. How does wasting paper hurt the environment?

3. What does Smith mean when he says, "You can do it all with one paper towel"? All what?

4. What does Smith mean when he says, "Next year, toilet paper." Why is this funny?

5. Will you try to follow Joe Smith's instructions next time you use a paper towel? Why, or why not?

I ▶ 1.4 EXPAND YOUR VOCABULARY Watch the excerpts from the TED Talk. Guess the meanings of the phrases in the box.

> kicks out   way too big   for the rest of your life   no small thing

J WATCH MORE Go to TED.com to watch the full TED Talk by Joe Smith.

Giant fish made from recycled plastic bottles on exhibit at a beach in Rio de Janeiro, Brazil

AFTER YOU WATCH

K **THINK CRITICALLY** **Interpret an Infographic.** Work in a group. Study the infographic. Then answer the questions. Use information from the infographic and your own ideas.

1. The purpose of the infographic is to encourage people to use _____ instead of paper.

2. According to this infographic, paper makes up _____ percent of all the waste Americans throw away every year.

3. What is an example of "unwanted mail"? What happens to the unwanted mail that Americans receive? What do you do with your unwanted mail?

4. What are other examples of paper that you throw away?

5. Why does the infographic mention "169 million trees"?

6. Do you receive any newspapers, catalogs, or magazines in the mail? Do you receive any digitally? Which do you prefer, and why?

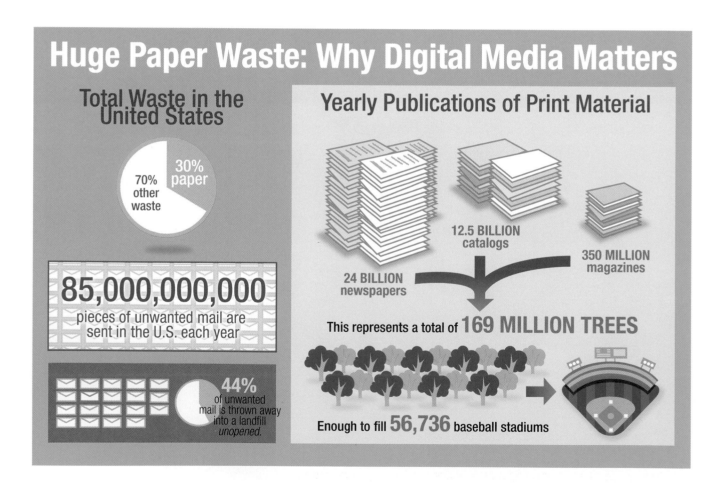

Huge Paper Waste: Why Digital Media Matters

Total Waste in the United States

30% paper
70% other waste

85,000,000,000 pieces of unwanted mail are sent in the U.S. each year

44% of unwanted mail is thrown away into a landfill unopened.

Yearly Publications of Print Material

24 BILLION newspapers
12.5 BILLION catalogs
350 MILLION magazines

This represents a total of 169 MILLION TREES

Enough to fill 56,736 baseball stadiums

Put It Together

A THINK CRITICALLY Synthesize. Work in small groups. Complete the chart. Add information from the interview in Part 1 and the TED Talk in Part 2. *Note: A resource is something we use to make or do something.*

	INTERVIEW: TIPS FOR SAVING WATER	TED TALK: HOW TO USE A PAPER TOWEL
1. Resource		
2. What are some ways we use the resource?		
3. How do we waste the resource?		
4. Tips for saving the resource		

B THINK CRITICALLY Personalize. Besides water and paper, what are some other resources or materials that people can try to conserve in order to help the environment? Share examples from your own life.

COMMUNICATE

ASSIGNMENT: Give a Group Presentation You will give a group presentation with tips for helping the environment. Review the ideas in Parts 1 and 2 and the listening and speaking skills as you prepare your presentation.

PREPARE

PRESENTATION SKILL Focus Your Topic

It is not possible to say everything about a subject in one short presentation. You usually need to focus your topic—talk about just one part of it. As you plan your presentation, ask yourself *wh*-questions to focus your topic. Here are some examples:

What resource will I talk about? **Water**

How can we conserve water? **Tips**

Where can we conserve water? **At home**

Compare the topics in the pyramid. The topic at the bottom is extremely general, and the one at the top is very focused. As you move up the pyramid, notice which *wh*-questions helped to focus the topic.

Tips for conserving water at home

Tips for conserving water

Conserving water

Conserving resources

C Work in a small group. Brainstorm a list of resources (e.g., electricity) or materials (e.g., plastic) that we should try to conserve to help the environment.

D Choose one resource or material. If necessary, focus the topic by asking *wh*-questions. Make sure you can discuss your topic in 4–5 minutes.

E Organize your presentation. Take notes in the outline.

    I. Introduction

       Resource or material: _____

    II. Body

       A. How we waste it: _____

          _____

       B. Why we need to save it: _____

          _____

       C. Tips for conserving it:

          1. _____

          2. _____

          3. _____

          4. _____

    III. Conclusion: _____

F COLLABORATE Use your outline. Decide who will present each part.

G Read the rubric on page 180 before you present. Notice how your presentation will be evaluated. Keep these categories in mind as you present and watch your classmates' presentations.

PRESENT

H Give your presentation to another small group. Watch your classmates' presentations. After you watch each one, provide feedback using the rubric as a guide. Add notes or any other feedback you want to share.

I THINK CRITICALLY Evaluate. In your group, discuss the feedback you received. As a class, discuss what each group did well and what might make each presentation even stronger.

REFLECT

Reflect on what you have learned. Check [✓] your progress.

I can
- [ ] listen for numbers and statistics.
- [ ] use a simple outline.
- [ ] give tips or suggestions.
- [ ] use correct syllable stress.
- [ ] focus a presentation topic.

I understand the meanings of these words and can use them.
Circle those you know. Underline those you need to work on.

(on) average	dispenser	invention	reduce	statistics **AWL**
conserve	figure	leak	require **AWL**	tear (off)
crucial **AWL**	fold	prove	resource **AWL**	waste
cut	huge	recycle	shake	wave

Answers for Exercise N, page 11:

1. False. The correct number is about 69%.
2. True.
3. True.
4. False. Fish need oxygen to live. If the water they are swimming in does not have enough oxygen, they can drown.
5. False. NASA has discovered water in the form of ice on the moon.
6. False. It takes 18 gallons.
7. True.
8. False. The opposite is true.
9. True.
10. False. The world record for holding one's breath underwater is 22 minutes.

UNIT 2
Connecting to Nature

Cheetahs taking a ride on a jeep on safari in Africa

THINK AND DISCUSS

1 Read the unit title. What does it mean?

2 Look at the photo and read the caption. How do you think the photo relates to the unit title? Explain.

Photos from a Safari

BEFORE YOU LISTEN

A COMMUNICATE Work in a small group. Discuss these questions.

1. Look at the map. Where is the Serengeti National Park?
2. Describe the photo. What is happening? How does it make you feel?
3. What is a *safari?* Share what you know about this experience.

B 1.9 THINK CRITICALLY Predict. You are going to hear a conversation between a man and a woman at work. The man has just returned from a safari in the Serengeti National Park. Listen to the first part of the conversation. Then answer these questions.

1. What kind of safari did the man go on?
2. How does the man describe his experience?
3. What will the man probably talk about next?

Serengeti National Park

A cheetah chases a wildebeest in Kenya.

VOCABULARY

C 🎧 **1.10** Read and listen to the sentences with words from the conversation. Guess the meaning of each bold word or phrase. Then write each word or phrase next to its definition.

a. Gayle and **a couple of** her friends decided to go camping, so they bought a tent for three people.

b. Tigers are **endangered** animals. We have to protect them before they disappear.

c. The **landscape** was flat and brown, with low hills in the distance.

d. My dog **chases** every cat he sees, but he never catches them.

e. There are only about 800 mountain gorillas in the world today. They are in serious danger of becoming **extinct.**

f. The seasons follow each other in an endless **cycle.**

g. The Amazon jungle is getting smaller because of human activity. **Conservation** is necessary to protect it.

h. If you're going to hike in the desert, it is **essential** to take lots of water with you.

i. The law protects elephants in Africa, but each day hunters kill hundreds of them **illegally.**

j. Akiko wants to get into the best university, so she has a strong **motivation** to study hard.

1. _____*cycle*_____ (n) events that happen again and again in the same order

2. _____ (adj) necessary; vital

3. _____ (n) two

4. _____ (n) desire or reason to do or accomplish something

5. _____ (v) runs after something to try to catch it

6. _____ (adv) in a way that is against the law

7. _____ (n) a far and wide view of land

8. _____ (adj) in danger of disappearing

9. _____ (adj) no longer existing

10. _____ (n) saving or preserving something, especially in nature

D COMMUNICATE Work with a partner. Take turns asking and answering the questions. Use the words in bold in your answers.

> A: *Describe the* **landscape** *where you live. For example, is it flat, or does it have hills? Are there trees or plants? If so, what kind?*
>
> B: *Near my home, the* **landscape** *is green and hilly. There are trees everywhere.*

1. Describe the **landscape** where you live. For example, is it flat, or does it have hills? What kind of trees and plants are there?

2. Which plants or animals in your area need **conservation** to survive?

3. What conditions are **essential** for workers to be happy in their jobs?

4. What are some ways that people can help save animals from becoming **extinct?**

5. If you park **illegally** in your area, what will happen?

6. What is your **motivation** for taking this class or course?

LISTEN

E 🎧 **1.11** ▶ **1.5** **LISTEN FOR MAIN IDEAS** Listen to the conversation. Answer the questions.

1. Why did Tom decide to go on a safari? Choose two reasons.
   a. He wanted to help catch poachers.   c. He wanted to see a rhino.
   b. He wanted to help conservation efforts.   d. He enjoys photography.

2. Look at Tom's photos. Number them in the order you hear them discussed in the conversation.

a. _____

b. _____

WORDS IN THE CONVERSATION
poaching (v): illegal catching or killing of wild animals

c. _____

d. _____

F 🎧 **1.11** **LISTEN FOR DETAILS** Listen again. Write T if a sentence is *true* and F if it is *false*. Then correct the false statements.

1. _____ Tom spent two weeks in the Serengeti.

2. _____ Today there are about 4,000 rhinos in the world.

3. _____ The Serengeti has a lot of hills.

4. _____ Tom's tour group traveled by jeep.

5. _____ A wildebeest is a kind of big cat.

6. _____ The lions attacked Tom's jeep.

7. _____ A cheetah can run faster than a gazelle.

8. _____ Tom tried to save the baby gazelle.

LISTENING SKILL Recognize a Speaker's Tone and Feeling

Tone is the way that speakers express their feelings or attitude about a topic. When speakers are excited, they usually speak faster and louder, and their voices rise. When they are sad or upset, they often speak softer and lower.

🎧 **1.12** Listen to the example from the conversation. Notice how Sharon's tone in the last sentence shows her excitement.

G 🎧 **1.13** Listen to segments from the conversation. Choose the word that describes how the speaker feels in each sentence below.

1. **Sharon:** "Really? What happened to them?"
   a. bored   **b.** shocked   **c.** curious

2. **Tom:** "Poaching! People killing them illegally."
   a. interested   **b.** excited   **c.** angry

3. **Tom:** "About a thousand."
   a. amused   **b.** worried   **c.** uninterested

4. **Sharon:** "Oh, no! How did it make you feel to see that?"
   a. happy   **b.** surprised   **c.** upset

5. **Tom:** "I . . . accepted it."
   a. excited   **b.** okay   **c.** upset

AFTER YOU LISTEN

H **THINK CRITICALLY** **Reflect.** Work in a group. Use information from exercises E, F, and G to discuss the questions.

1. In the conversation, Tom gives two reasons for going on a safari in the Serengeti National Park. Do you think these are good reasons to go on a safari? Why, or why not?

2. Why does it matter if one endangered animal or plant disappears?

3. Why does poaching happen? How can governments prevent it?

4. Tom says, "[Nature is] an endless cycle, and we're just a tiny part of it." What do you think he means?

SPEAKING

SPEAKING SKILL **Use Descriptive Language**

Speakers use descriptive language to help their listeners imagine and better understand how a person, place, or thing looks, sounds, smells, feels, or behaves. Two kinds of descriptive language are descriptive adjectives and descriptive details.

Descriptive adjectives:

a **photo** safari   **tall** grass   It was **awesome**.

Descriptive details:

trees **that look like umbrellas**   animals **with horns**

I 🎧 **1.14** Work with a partner. Listen to the segments from the conversation. Then answer the questions with descriptive language.

Segment 1

1. What kind of guide led Tom's tour? _____

2. What did the jeeps look like? _____

3. Where did the tour group sleep? _____

Segment 2

4. What kind of lions did the tourists see? _____

5. Where were the lions? _____

6. What were the lions doing? _____

7. Where did the jeep stop? _____

8. How long did the tourists watch the lions? _____

J **COMMUNICATE** Work with a partner. Each student chooses a photo from pages 26 or 27 and describes it using descriptive details and adjectives.

> A: *The landscape is very flat. The grass is yellow and green.*

PRONUNCIATION SKILL Thought Groups and Pausing

English speakers divide speech into meaningful segments, or *thought groups*. In writing, punctuation often indicates the end of an idea or thought. In speaking, we pause at the end of an idea or thought. Read and listen to the example from the conversation. Notice the thought groups and pauses.

🎧 **1.15** *Hey, Tom! / Welcome back! / How was your vacation?*

Speakers may divide a sentence differently depending on what ideas and thoughts are important to them.

K 🎧 **1.16** Listen to the sentences from the conversation. Put a slash (/) at the end of each thought group.

1. The main point was that countries like Kenya and Tanzania rely on tourism to pay for wildlife conservation.

2. It covers five thousand seven hundred square miles.

3. Here's a picture I took at a drinking hole early one morning.

4. They're members of the antelope family. They look kind of scary, don't you think?

5. One afternoon, we were driving along, and we saw these two female lions lying in the middle of the road, asleep.

6. So our guide stopped the jeep about 10 feet away, and we just sat there watching them for about 15 minutes.

7. Animals like gazelles eat grass, and then animals like cheetahs eat gazelles.

L 🎧 **1.16** Listen again and repeat the sentences in exercise K.

M Work with a partner. Choose a part, A or B, in the conversation below. Divide the sentences for your part into thought groups. Then read the conversations aloud.

1. A: Hey, Tom! Welcome back! How was your vacation?

   B: It was . . . awesome.

   A: Oh, yeah? Where did you go?

   B: I went to the Serengeti National Park. I spent 10 days on a photo safari.

   A: Wow! What made you decide to do that?

   B: Well, there were a couple of reasons.

2. A: It's so green.

   B: Yeah, April is the rainy season. It rained every day on my trip.

   A: Did you travel alone, or did you go with a guide?

   B: I went on a group tour with a professional guide. We traveled in jeeps with seven seats, and at night we slept in tents in a camp.

N **THINK CRITICALLY Interpret an Infographic.** Work in a small group. Study the infographic about endangered African animals. Discuss your answers to these questions.

1. Why are the animals different colors? _____

2. If an animal image is facing left, it means the animal population is (increasing / decreasing). If the image is facing right, it means the population is (increasing / decreasing).

3. According to the infographic, how many species of animals are endangered? _____

4. What is the status of the red animals? _____

5. What is the status of the green animals? _____

6. What is the status of elephants? _____

7. What is the status of humans? Why do you think humans are included here?

   _____

8. Does any of the information surprise you? Explain.

The International Union for Conservation of Nature divides species into five categories. "Critically Endangered" means the species is almost extinct. "Least Concern" means the species is not in danger.

ENDANGERED SAFARI

Critically Endangered
Endangered
Vulnerable
Near Threatened
Least Concern

Decreasing | Stable or Increasing
Population

data from v2014.3
The IUCN Red List of Threatened Species

INFO WE TRUST
©2015 RJ Andrews. All rights reserved.

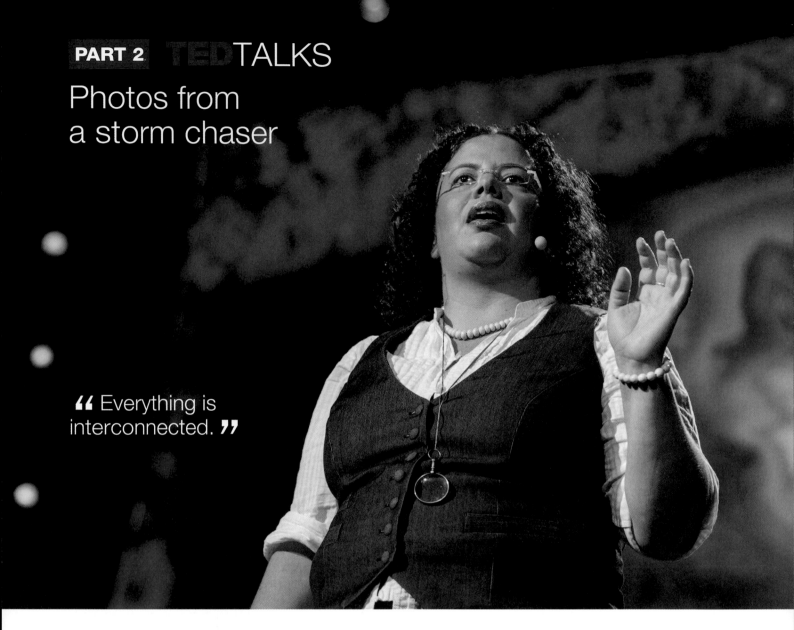

Photos from
a storm chaser

" Everything is
interconnected. **"**

BEFORE YOU WATCH

A THINK CRITICALLY Predict. Read the title and information about the TED
speaker. What is a *storm*? Can you guess what a *storm chaser* does? What do you
think Seaman will talk about?

CAMILLE SEAMAN Photographer

Camille Seaman takes photographs all over the world using digital and film
cameras. In addition to her photographs of clouds, she has photographed
icebergs in the Arctic and Antarctic. Another one of her photography projects
shows the beauty of natural environments in Siberia.

Camille Seaman's idea worth spreading is that we should find ways to
experience the natural forces that connect everything on the planet.

B Read the following statements. Write A if you agree and D if you disagree.

1. _____ I am surprised Camille Seaman enjoys chasing storms.

2. _____ Storm chasing requires special equipment.

3. _____ Storm chasing is dangerous.

4. _____ Storm chasing is exciting.

5. _____ I would like to try storm chasing.

C COMMUNICATE Work with a partner. Discuss your answers to exercise B.

A: *I don't want to try storm chasing. I think it would be too dangerous.*

B: *True. But it would also be really exciting! I'd like to try it.*

National Geographic Explorer and severe-storm researcher Tim Samaras chasing a storm in North Dakota, U.S.

VOCABULARY

D 🎧 **1.17** The sentences below will help you learn words in the TED Talk. Read and listen to the sentences. Then choose the meaning of each word or phrase in bold.

1. Bees and flowers are **interconnected.** One cannot live without the other one.
   a. related to each other
   b. found everywhere
   c. made from the same material

2. While working in the hot sun, I **perspired** so much that my shirt got all wet.
   a. felt tired
   b. sweated
   c. got bored

3. The photos and diagrams **illustrate** how clouds form.
   a. explain
   b. draw
   c. understand

4. A tornado is so powerful that it **is capable of** lifting cars and throwing them in the air.
   a. enjoys
   b. expects
   c. has the ability

5. Even from a distance of five miles, the tornado was a **spectacular** sight.
   a. dangerous
   b. awesome
   c. large

6. The tornado traveled in a **straight** line for 10 miles, and then it turned suddenly in a different direction.
   a. without turns or curves
   b. correct
   c. thick

7. Last summer, Tim **witnessed** a tornado for the first time. "It was a sight I will never forget," he said.
   a. believed
   b. caused
   c. saw

8. Millions of years ago, powerful **forces** pushed up the earth and created the Rocky Mountains.
   a. winds
   b. natural powers
   c. storms

9. Planting a vegetable garden is a simple **process** with easy-to-follow instructions.

  a. decision

  b. series of steps

  c. action

10. The universe probably includes millions of **planets** like our Earth.

  a. human beings

  b. plants and animals

  c. objects that travel around a star

E COMMUNICATE Work with a partner. Take turns asking and answering the questions.

> A: *How many miles **are** you **capable of** running?*
>
> B: *None! I don't like to run.*

1. How many miles **are** you **capable of** running?

2. How are humans, animals, and plants **interconnected?**

3. In your family, who has **straight** hair? Who has curly hair?

4. Do you believe there are other **planets** like Earth in the universe? Why, or why not?

5. What is your **process** for learning new vocabulary?

6. Have you ever **witnessed** a crime or an accident? Describe it.

7. What is one of the most **spectacular** sights you have ever seen?

WATCH

F ▶ **1.6** **WATCH FOR MAIN IDEAS** Read the statements. Then watch the TED Talk. Check [✓] the sentence that expresses the main idea of the talk.

1. _____ As a Shinnecock Indian, Seaman lives near the town of Southampton, New York.

2. _____ Seaman began storm chasing because her daughter encouraged her to do it.

3. _____ Seaman uses photographs to illustrate the idea that everything in nature is connected to everything else.

4. _____ Seaman's grandfather taught her that humans and clouds are formed by the same natural forces.

WORDS IN THE TALK
hail (n): frozen rain that falls in small balls from the sky
lightning (n): flashes of light in the sky during a storm
tactile (adj): related to the sense of touch

learnmore Camille Seaman says she is a Shinnecock Indian. Nowadays Indians are also called *Native Americans.* These are the people who lived in North America before the Europeans arrived in the 15th century. Traditionally, Native Americans lived in large groups called *tribes.*

NOTE-TAKING SKILL Use Abbreviations and Symbols

When you take notes on a talk or lecture, you don't have time to write all the speaker's words. You can save time if you use abbreviations and symbols.

Speaker's words: *We are a small fishing tribe situated on the southeastern tip of Long Island.*

Notes: we = sm fish. tribe on SE tip of L. Isld.

One way to abbreviate words is to write only the consonants within them:

everything → evrthng   fishing → fshng   grandfather → grndfthr

Another way is to use common abbreviations, such as these, for some of the words in the talk:

New York → NY   feet → ft   miles → m   photograph → photo

Here are some common symbols you can use in your notes:

is, are, equals =	up, go up ↑
more than, bigger than >	down, go down ↓
less than, smaller than <	percent %
cause, lead to, make, become, or produce →	

You should use symbols and abbreviations that *you* understand.

G ▶ **1.7** **WATCH FOR DETAILS** Watch excerpts of the TED Talk. Complete the notes. Use abbreviations and symbols from the skill box or create your own. You may use the same symbol more than once.

1. Everything _____ interconnected

2. Your water _____ cloud _____ rain

3. Super-cell clouds:

huge hail + _____ tornadoes; _____ do

_____ 50 _____ wide

_____ 65,000 _____ high

H COMMUNICATE With a partner, compare your answers to exercise G. Then use your notes to retell the information you heard in the TED Talk.

> A: *Super cell clouds can grow to be really big, but only a small percent produce tornadoes.*

I ▶ **1.8 WATCH FOR DETAILS** Watch excerpts of the TED Talk again. Fill in the blanks with descriptive adjectives from the box. Use a dictionary if necessary.

> charged   spectacular   super   turquoise
> giant   straight   tactile   warm
> grapefruit

1. "And so three days later, driving very fast, I found myself stalking a single type of _____ cloud called the _____ cell, capable of producing _____ -size hail and _____ tornadoes, although only two percent actually do."

2. "Storm chasing is a very _____ experience. There's a _____, moist wind blowing at your back and the smell of the earth, the wheat, the grass, the _____ particles. And then there are the colors in the clouds of hail forming, the greens and the _____ blues. I've learned to respect the lightning. My hair used to be _____."

J ▶ **1.9 EXPAND YOUR VOCABULARY** Watch the excerpts from the TED Talk. Guess the meanings of the words and phrases in the box.

> after a while   stalking   I'm kidding   small-scale version

AFTER YOU WATCH

K THINK CRITICALLY Infer. Work with a partner. Discuss these questions.

1. Seaman says, "Everything is interconnected. As a Shinnecock Indian, I was raised to know this." What does she mean? What is "this"?

2. What example did Seaman's grandfather use to teach her the lesson in question 1? Can you think of another example?

3. Why did Seaman start chasing storms?

4. Seaman says, "I've learned to respect the lightning." Why does she say this?

5. Why does Seaman compare storm clouds to "lovely monsters"?

6. Do Seaman's photos make you think differently about nature? Why, or why not?

A storm chaser captures
an image of a tornado

L COLLABORATE Work in a small group. Look at the photo taken by a storm chaser. Imagine that you are standing in this person's place. Use descriptive language to talk about what you see, hear, feel, and smell.

A: *The building under the cloud looks like a mouse under an elephant.*

Put It Together

A **THINK CRITICALLY Synthesize.** Work in a small group. Complete the chart with information from the conversation in Part 1 and the TED Talk in Part 2.

Questions	Conversation: Photos from a Safari	TED Talk: Photos from a storm chaser
1. What was the setting? (place and time)		
2. What activity(ies) does the speaker describe?		
3. Why does the speaker do it?		
4. How does the speaker describe the experience?		
5. What makes the speaker feel connected to nature?		

B **THINK CRITICALLY Personalize.** Work with a partner. Compare your answers in exercise A. Which experience would you prefer to have—a safari or storm chasing? Why?

COMMUNICATE

ASSIGNMENT: Give an Individual Presentation You will give an individual presentation about a time when you felt a special connection to nature. Review the ideas in Parts 1 and 2 and the listening and speaking skills as you prepare your presentation.

PREPARE

PRESENTATION SKILL Use Visual Aids

Your presentations will be more interesting for your audience if you illustrate them with visual aids—drawings, photographs, video clips, charts, slides, maps, and even physical objects. Here are some tips for using visual aids effectively:

- Introduce your visual aid. Explain what it is. Make sure your audience knows why you are showing it.

- Use bright, clear, simple images.

- Make your visual aid large enough for everyone in the room to see.

- If you use slides with text, keep the phrases short and simple. Don't read from your slides.

- Look at your audience while you are talking, not at your visual aid.

▶ **1.10** Watch an excerpt from the TED Talk. Notice how Seaman uses beautiful, clear photographs to make her presentation more interesting.

(See page 177 in the *Independent Student Handbook* for more information on using visual aids in presentations.)

C Complete the outline to organize your talk. Don't write sentences. Write key words and use symbols and abbreviations.

    I. Introduction

        A. Setting

            Where? _____

            When? _____

        B. Activity: _____

        C. Why did you do it (1–2 reasons)?

            _____

            _____

        D. Describe the experience. Use descriptive language.

            _____

            _____

            _____

        E. What made you feel connected to nature?

            _____

D Choose your visual aid. Decide where in the talk you will show it and what you will say about it.

E Work with a partner. Practice your presentation aloud, using your outline and your visual aid.

F Read the rubric on page 180 before you present. Notice how your presentation will be evaluated. Keep these categories in mind as you present and watch your classmates' presentations.

PRESENT

G Give your presentation to a small group. Watch your classmates' presentations. After you watch each one, provide feedback using the rubric as a guide. Add notes and any other feedback you want to share.

H **THINK CRITICALLY Evaluate.** In a small group, discuss the feedback you received. Discuss what you did well and what might make your presentation even stronger.

REFLECT

Reflect on what you have learned. Check [✓] your progress.

I can
- ☐ recognize a speaker's tone and feeling.
- ☐ use descriptive language.
- ☐ use thought groups and pausing.
- ☐ take notes using abbreviations and symbols.
- ☐ use a visual aid during a presentation.

I understand the meanings of these words and can use them.
Circle those you know. Underline those you need to work on.

a couple of `AWL`	cycle `AWL`	force	landscape	process `AWL`
(be) capable (of) `AWL`	endangered	illegally `AWL`	motivation `AWL`	spectacular
chase	essential	illustrate `AWL`	perspire	straight
conservation	extinct	interconnected	planet	witness

UNIT 3
Going Places

Gigantic Sultan's Elephant—a moving
sculpture in Nantes, France

1 Read the unit title. What do you think of when you hear the phrase *going places*?

2 Describe the photo. What do you see?

3 How do you think the photo relates to the title? Explain.

PART 1 No Car, No Worries

BEFORE YOU LISTEN

A COMMUNICATE Work in a small group. Discuss these questions.

1. Look at the photo. Describe it. Where do you think it was taken?

2. What are some transportation problems related to cars?

3. Is transportation a problem for you? Explain.

B 🎧 **1.18 COMMUNICATE** You are going to hear a panel discussion about three methods of transportation. A *panel* is a group of people who discuss different aspects of a topic. Listen to the introduction. What does the speaker say about cars? What are *alternative* methods of transportation? Can you give examples? Discuss your ideas with your group.

Traffic in Xiamen, China

VOCABULARY

C 🎧 **1.19** Read and listen to the sentences with words from the panel discussion. Guess the meaning of each bold word. Then write each word next to its definition.

a. "Hello. I'm taking a **survey** about transportation. Can I ask you some questions?"

b. This sports car has a powerful engine. It has the **capacity** to go from 0 to 100 miles per hour in 30 seconds.

c. The newest electric cars have a **range** of about 200 miles before the battery dies.

d. The weather report says there is a 100 percent chance of snow tonight. I **definitely** won't ride my bike to work tomorrow.

e. Public transportation is a **convenient** way to get to work because you don't have to worry about parking.

f. To get downtown their are several **alternatives**. You can take the subway, the trolley, or a bus.

g. The street is very **narrow**. There isn't enough room for two cars to pass.

h. My cell phone is almost dead. I need to **charge** the battery.

i. The building has a complicated security **system**. It uses many types of locks, gates, and cameras.

j. One **benefit** of riding my bike to work is that I don't have to waste time waiting for a bus.

1. _____ *narrow* _____ (adj) thin, not wide

2. _____ (adv) certainly; absolutely; for sure

3. _____ (n) the distance that a car, truck, etc. can go without running out of fuel

4. _____ (n) a set of questions about people's opinions, habits, etc.

5. _____ (n) advantage; positive result

6. _____ (adj) easy and comfortable to use or do

7. _____ (n) ability to do something

8. _____ (n) choices

9. _____ (n) a group of related parts that work or move together

10. _____ (v) put electricity into a battery

D COMMUNICATE Work with a partner. Take turns reading the statements. Tell your partner if the statement is true for you. Explain why, or why not.

> A: *Statement one is true for me. I will **definitely** buy an electric car someday. I plan to buy one next year.*
>
> B: *Really? I have never really thought about it.*

1. I will **definitely** buy an electric car someday.

2. I enjoy taking **surveys** online.

3. I have a good **system** for learning new words.

4. I live in a **convenient** area. There is shopping and transportation nearby.

5. I would enjoy riding a bicycle down a **narrow** mountain road.

6. One **benefit** of my home is that it is close to school.

7. I **charge** my cell phone every day.

LISTEN

LISTENING SKILL Listen for Signposts

Signposts are words and phrases that tell listeners what a speaker is going to talk about. There are many different kinds of signposts. Here are some common signposts, or signals, that speakers use for introducing a topic or moving to a new topic.

Common signposts for introducing a topic:

I'm going to talk about . . .   *My topic is . . .*
I plan to discuss . . .   *I'm going to present . . .*

Common signposts for moving to a new topic:

Next,   *Also,*   *In addition,*

1.18 Notice the signposts in the introduction to the panel discussion.

Let's start with a little survey.

Today we're going to talk about three alternative methods that are ecofriendly, fast, and efficient.

Miguel will speak first.

E 🎧 **1.20 LISTEN FOR MAIN IDEAS** Listen to the speakers introduce their topics. Write the signposts they use and the methods of transportation they will discuss.

Speaker	Signpost	Method of Transportation
1. Miguel		
2. Jean		
3. Yulia		

NOTE-TAKING SKILL **Indent Details**

When you take notes, put each new piece of information on a separate line. Put main ideas or topics on the left side of your paper. *Indent*, or move, details to the right. Keep moving to the right as details become more specific. Look at the example about car sharing, a rental system that allows people to rent cars for short periods of time. Notice the abbreviations and symbols.

Benefits of car sharing

    Saves money

        30% of ppl who used car sharing sold their car

        saved $300-400 a mo.

    Helps environment

        reduces # of cars on road ⟶ less pollution

        don't look for parking

F 🎧 **1.21** ▶ **1.11 LISTEN FOR DETAILS** Listen to segment 1 of the panel discussion. Write the missing details. Remember to indent.

Problems w/ travel to/from El Alto & La Paz

    took a long time

Benefits of Mi Teleférico system

G 🎧 **1.22** ▶ **1.12** **LISTEN FOR DETAILS** Listen to segment 2 of the panel discussion. Write the missing details.

1. Ebikes can travel _____ miles per hour.

2. They have a battery range of about _____ miles.

3. In the U.S. an electric bike costs between $_____ and $ _____.

4. It costs _____ cents to charge the battery.

5. It costs less than _____ per mile.

H 🎧 **1.23** ▶ **1.13** Read the statements. Then listen to segment 3 of the panel discussion. Write T for *true* or F for *false*. Then correct the false statements.

1. _____ By definition, microcars have seats for just two people.

2. _____ All microcars have three wheels.

3. _____ Today, some microcars use gasoline.

4. _____ The Tango is an electric car.

5. _____ The Tango is the world's shortest car.

AFTER YOU LISTEN

I **THINK CRITICALLY Infer.** Work in groups. Discuss these questions. Use information from the panel discussion to support your answers.

1. What are other benefits of each type of transportation discussed?

2. What are some disadvantages of each type?

3. What transportation problems are there in your city or area? Could the types of transportation in the panel discussion help to fix any of these problems? How?

SPEAKING

SPEAKING SKILL **Use Listing Signals**

Listing signals are words and phrases that you can use to help your listener follow the organization of your talk. For example:

Electric bicycles have three big advantages. **First,** . . .

Another *advantage of microcars is that they are easy to park.*

Here are some useful listing signals:

- *First, first of all, the first (noun), to start, to begin*

- *Second, secondly, the second, next, another, also*

- *Last, the last, finally*

J COMMUNICATE Work with a partner. Study the outline below with information about the Tango car. Choose three places where you can add listing signals. Then take turns giving the information. You can begin like this:

> A: *The Tango car has three big advantages.* **To begin,** *it is very small.*

I. Advantages

    A. Small size

        1. 8 feet, 6 inches long

        2. 39 inches wide = narrowest car in the world

        3. room for two passengers, one behind the other

    B. Range: 100 miles per charge

    C. Speed: Up to 120 miles per hour

A Tango electric microcar

Intonation is the way your voice rises (goes up) and falls (goes down) when you speak. In English, a speaker's intonation usually rises a little on the last stressed syllable of every thought group. At the end of the final thought group of a statement, the speaker's intonation falls. This indicates that the sentence or idea is finished. Read and listen to the examples.

1.24

My city is in a valley / with mountains all around. /

An ebike / is basically a regular bike / with a motor and a battery. /

K **1.25** Listen to sentences with information from the panel discussion. Insert a rising–falling arrow to show the intonation pattern of each thought group.

1. The Teleférico / operates on electricity. /

2. The Teleférico / has the capacity / to carry 600 passengers / a day. /

3. Most ebikes / can travel 20 / or 30 / miles per hour. /

4. Ebikes are expensive to buy, / but they're cheap to operate. /

5. Microcars / are the smallest cars / on the road. /

6. The Tango car / has seats / for only two people. /

L **1.25** Listen again and check your answers from exercise K. Then with a partner, take turns saying the sentences.

M **COLLABORATE** Work with a partner. Write three sentences about the methods of transportation from the panel discussion. Show your sentences to a partner. Your partner will say your sentences with rising-falling intonation.

_____

_____

_____

_____

N COMMUNICATE Use the information in the chart to ask questions. If someone answers *Yes* to your question, write his or her name in the chart.

A: *Do you walk to school?*

B: *Yes, I do.*

Find someone who . . .	Name
walks to school	
has ridden a cable car	
would like to buy an ebike	
takes two buses to school or work	
owns a car	
carpools to school or work	
uses a service like Uber or Lyft	
thinks microcars are dangerous	
uses a bicycle for transportation	

Women riding an electric-powered bicycle, Beijing, China

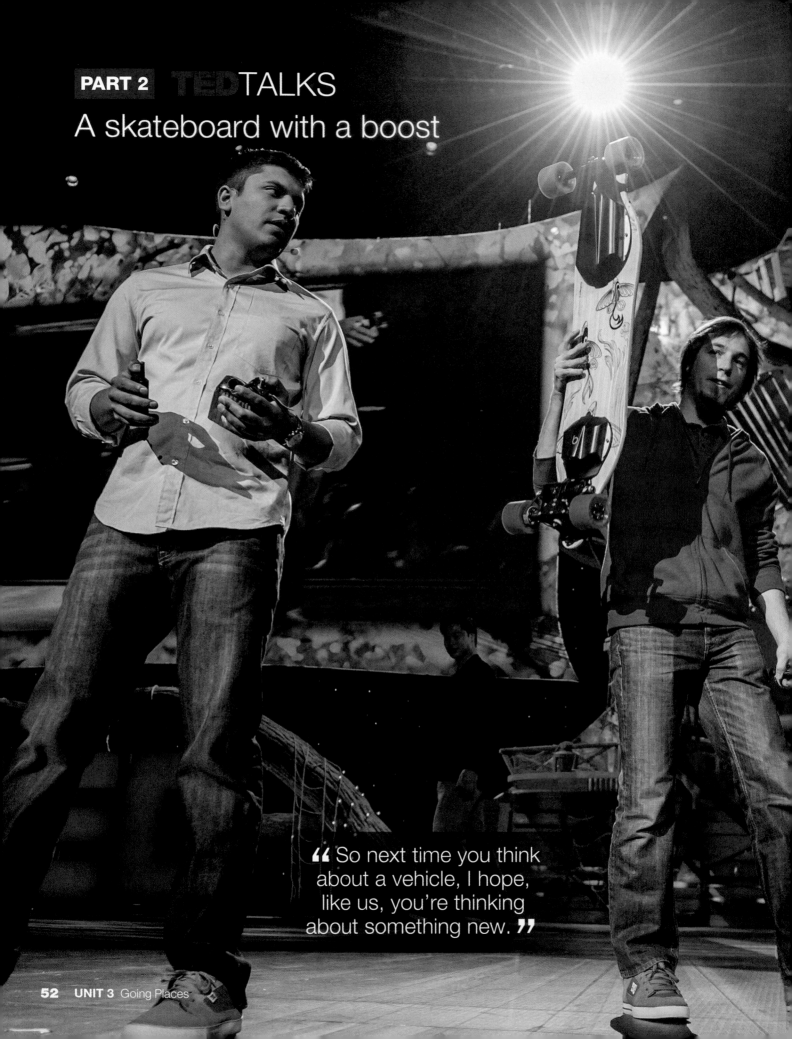

A skateboard with a boost

❝ So next time you think about a vehicle, I hope, like us, you're thinking about something new. **❞**

BEFORE YOU WATCH

A **THINK CRITICALLY Predict.** Read the title and the information about the TED speaker. A *boost* is an increase or improvement in something. What do you think the speaker will talk about? Tell your class.

> ### SANJAY DASTOOR Roboticist
>
> Sanjay Dastoor holds a PhD in robotics from Stanford University. While he was at Stanford, he and two friends often talked about the need for a better way to get around campus. So they created an electric longboard and started a company called Boosted Boards. This Silicon Valley company hopes to provide a new way to commute for people who live close to work.
>
> Sanjay Dastoor's idea worth spreading is that with a little creative thinking, you can turn an everyday object like a skateboard into a quick and ecofriendly way to get around the city.

B **COMMUNICATE** Read the following statements. Check [✓] the ones that you agree with.

1. _____ I have or would like to have a skateboard.

2. _____ Riding a skateboard is a fun hobby.

3. _____ Riding a skateboard can be dangerous.

4. _____ A skateboard is a useful form of transportation.

5. _____ Anyone can ride a skateboard.

C **COMMUNICATE** Work with a partner. Discuss the statements you checked in exercise B.

VOCABULARY

D 🎧 **1.26** These sentences will help you learn words in the TED Talk. Read and listen to the sentences. Guess the meaning of each word in bold. Then write each word next to its definition on page 54.

a. If you ride a bicycle, be sure to look for **vehicles** before you cross the street.

b. We need three different **remote controls** to operate our television.

c. I have an opinion, but I would like to hear your **perspective** about the plan.

d. It's a simple machine. It has only four **components**, so it's easy to build.

e. One advantage of this bicycle is its **portability**. I can pick it up and carry it on the train.

f. In a car with a gasoline engine, we control **acceleration** by pushing on the gas pedal with our foot.

g. The child sat in the corner by herself and did not **interact** with the other children in the room.

h. I'm not happy with the **performance** of this phone. I expected it to be faster.

i. The driving teacher told me to put my car in **reverse** and look behind me before backing up.

j. Petroleum is not a **sustainable** fuel. We need to start using clean alternatives, such as solar power.

1. _____interact_____ (v) act together and have an effect on each other

2. _____ (n) way of thinking about something; point of view

3. _____ (n) the quality of being able to be carried easily

4. _____ (n) the increase in speed of a thing that is moving

5. _____ (n) machines with wheels, such as a cars or buses, that are used for transportation

6. _____ (n) the parts used to build a machine or device

7. _____ (adj) able to continue for a long time without damaging the environment

8. _____ (n) the speed and efficiency of a machine, person, etc.

9. _____ (n) a backward direction (opposite of *forward*)

10. _____ (n) small, handheld devices for operating electronic equipment from a distance

E COMMUNICATE Work with a partner. Take turns asking and answering these questions.

A: *Have you ever been a passenger in an electric **vehicle**?*

B: *Yes. I've ridden in an electric golf cart.*

1. Have you ever been a passenger in an electric **vehicle**? What kind?

2. How many **remote controls** do you have? What do you use them for?

3. I think 16-year-olds are too young to drive. What is your **perspective** on this?

4. At a party, do you prefer to talk to your friends or to **interact** with new people?

5. Have you bought a new appliance or device lately? What was it? Are you satisfied with its **performance**? Why, or why not?

6. Have you ever hit anything behind you when your vehicle was in **reverse**?

7. Is the population of your country growing quickly or slowly? Is this growth rate **sustainable**?

8. Is it important for a vehicle to have fast **acceleration**? Why, or why not?

WATCH

F ▶ **1.14 WATCH FOR MAIN IDEAS** Read the list of topics. Then watch the TED Talk. Match each topic with the correct sign post phrase.

Topics	Signposts
a. sustainability	**1.** _____ Today I'm going to show you …
b. components of the skateboard motor	**2.** _____ So we built something.
c. the skateboard as a type of vehicle	**3.** _____ So today we're going to show you …
d. portability of the skateboard	**4.** _____ So we're going to show you …
e. maneuverability of the skateboard	**5.** _____ So I'll leave you with …

WORDS IN THE TALK

maneuverable (adj): easy to move or change position

Riding a boosted skateboard
up a hill in San Francisco, CA

G ▶1.15 **WATCH FOR DETAILS** Watch segment 1 of the TED Talk. Complete the sentences.

1. Dastoor's skateboard weighs _____ than a bicycle.

2. You can _____ it anywhere.

3. You can charge it in _____ minutes.

4. It can run for _____ kilometers on a _____ of electricity.

H ▶1.16 **WATCH FOR DETAILS** Watch segment 2 of the TED Talk. Complete the outline with the information in the box. Remember to indent the details.

20 mph uphill	6 miles of range	bought at a toy store
from remote control airplanes	~~motor~~	battery

Components
    Motor

_____

_____

_____

_____

_____

I ▶1.17 **WATCH FOR DETAILS** Read the statements. Then watch segment 3 of the TED Talk. Write T for *true*, F for *false*, or N for *not mentioned* for each statement. Then correct the false statements.

1. _____ The skateboard uses 10 times less energy than a car.

2. _____ You can buy it in a bicycle shop.

3. _____ The board cannot travel in reverse.

4. _____ It reduces the footprint of your energy use.

5. _____ It is fun to ride.

J ▶1.18 **EXPAND YOUR VOCABULARY** Watch the excerpts from the TED Talk. Guess the meanings of the words and phrases in the box.

wall outlet	novel concepts	handheld	compelling facts

AFTER YOU WATCH

K THINK CRITICALLY Reflect. Work with a partner. Discuss your answers to these questions.

1. How can a boosted board "change the way you interact with a city like San Francisco," to use Sanjay Dastoor's words? Do you think a boosted board could change the way you interact with the place where you live? How?

2. What might be some problems with using a boosted skateboard?

3. Who would probably feel comfortable riding a boosted board? Who might not feel as comfortable?

4. Think of an existing transportation method. Can you think of a creative way to make it better? How?

5. What form of transportation is your favorite? Why?

learnmore A *footprint* is the mark made by your foot when you step on the ground. However, when we talk about the environment, *footprint* means the amount of land, energy, water, etc. that a person or organization uses in order to exist or operate. *Carbon footprint* is the amount of carbon dioxide created when people or machines use fossil fuels such as petroleum. Driving your car increases your carbon footprint.

L THINK CRITICALLY Interpret an Infographic. Work in a group. Study the infographic below. Then answer these questions.

1. How does this infographic measure the amount of carbon that different types of transportation create?

2. The title asks, "How should you travel to reduce your carbon footprint?" What are the best ways, according to the infographic? What is the worst?

3. A train is very large; a scooter is very small. Why does a train have a smaller carbon footprint than a scooter?

4. In this unit, you learned about four types of transportation: cable cars, ebikes, electric microcars, and boosted skateboards. Where do you think each of these vehicles belongs on the infographic? What information helped you decide?

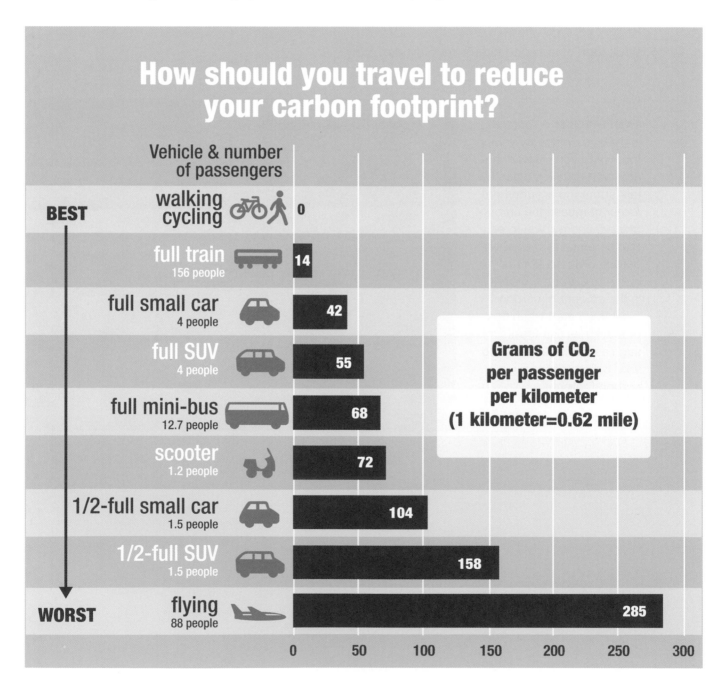

How should you travel to reduce your carbon footprint?

Vehicle & number of passengers

BEST

walking cycling		0
full train 156 people		14
full small car 4 people		42
full SUV 4 people		55
full mini-bus 12.7 people		68
scooter 1.2 people		72
1/2-full small car 1.5 people		104
1/2-full SUV 1.5 people		158
flying 88 people		285

WORST

Grams of CO₂ per passenger per kilometer (1 kilometer=0.62 mile)

0   50   100   150   200   250   300

Put It Together

A **THINK CRITICALLY** **Synthesize.** Work with a partner. Use the Venn diagram to compare the benefits of an ebike, a microcar, and a boosted skateboard. Consider these points: range, speed, cost to build or buy, cost to charge, and sustainability. Add your own ideas.

B **THINK CRITICALLY** **Reflect.** Discuss these questions with a partner.

1. Which type of transportation do you think has the most benefits?

2. Which type of transportation meets your needs the best? Why?

COMMUNICATE

ASSIGNMENT: Participate in a Panel Discussion You will participate in a panel discussion about three ecofriendly methods of transportation. Review the ideas in Parts 1 and 2 and the listening and speaking skills as you prepare for your discussion.

PREPARE

C COLLABORATE Work in a group of three. Each student chooses a different topic. Choose from the list below or use your own idea.

Abra	hoverboard	Shweeb system
car or bike sharing	jet pack	Skytrain
city cars, e.g., Smart car	Maglev train	sled
ELF vehicle	SCARAB	unicycle
ferry	scooter	Velomobile
flying bike	Segway	zipline
golf cart	self-driving car	other: _____

D Complete the outline with notes for your part of the panel discussion.

I. Topic: _____

    A. Description (e.g., range, cost, etc.)

       _____

       _____

       _____

       _____

    B. Benefits (e.g., speed, comfort, etc.)

       _____

       _____

       _____

       _____

PRESENTATION SKILL Rehearse Your Presentation

Before speaking in front of a group, rehearse your presentation aloud.

- Make an outline of your presentation. Practice looking up from your notes frequently to make eye contact with your audience.

- Memorize at least the first few sentences and last few sentences of your presentation.

- If possible, practice in front of a mirror. Think about how you will control nervous gestures such as touching your hair or twisting your hands. (See pages 177–178 of the *Independent Student Handbook* for more tips on preparing for a presentation.)

E COLLABORATE Rehearse your panel discussion. Use your outline. As you rehearse, use listing signals and correct statement intonation..

F Read the rubric on page 181 before you present. Notice how your panel discussion will be evaluated. Keep these categories in mind as you have your discussion and watch your classmates' discussion.

PRESENT

G Have your panel discussion in front of the class. Watch your classmates' discussion. After you watch each one, provide feedback using the rubric as a guide. Add notes and any other feedback you want to share.

H THINK CRITICALLY Evaluate. With the members of your panel, discuss the feedback you received. Discuss what you did well and what might make your panel discussion stronger.

REFLECT

Reflect on what you have learned. Check [✓] your progress.

I can
- [ ] listen for signposts.
- [ ] indent details when taking notes.
- [ ] use listing signals.
- [ ] use rising-falling intonation in statements.
- [ ] rehearse before giving a presentation.

I understand the meanings of these words and can use them.
Circle those you know. Underline those you need to work on.

acceleration	component AWL	performance	reverse AWL
alternative AWL	convenient	perspective AWL	survey AWL
benefit AWL	definitely AWL	portability	sustainable AWL
capacity AWL	interact AWL	range AWL	system
charge	narrow	remote control	vehicle AWL

UNIT 4
Music, Music Everywhere

A girl playing the piano in the back
of a truck in Arkansas, U.S.

THINK AND DISCUSS

1 Read the unit title. Do you believe that music is everywhere? Why, or why not?

2. Look at the photo and read the caption. Where is the girl? What is she doing? Where is the piano? Why do you think it is there?

BEFORE YOU LISTEN

A COMMUNICATE Work in a small group. Discuss these questions.

1. How important is music in your life?

2. How often do you listen to music?

3. Do you play an instrument? If yes, what do you play?

4. Do you like to sing? If yes, where do you sing?

B COLLABORATE You are going to hear an interview. In the interview, people talk about different types of music. Below are a few examples of types of music. Work in a group. Brainstorm more types. Think of as many as you can. Then share your list with the class.

Types of Music

classical   _____   _____

hip-hop   _____   _____

_____   _____   _____

Musicians taking a break in the Emilia-Romanga region of Italy

VOCABULARY

C 🎧 **1.27** Read and listen to the sentences with words from the interview. Choose the meaning of each bold word or phrase.

1. Some people really **focus** when they listen to music. They think about the music, and they don't do anything else.

   Focus means:
   a. pay attention
   b. become calm
   c. see better

2. Beautiful music **transports** some people. It can inspire their emotions.

   Transports means:
   a. improves one's hearing
   b. provides strong feelings
   c. creates confusion

3. Some people think live music is more **entertaining** than recorded music. They like to see the musicians play their instruments.

   Entertaining means:
   a. educational
   b. boring
   c. enjoyable

4. Pop music is a big **category.** It includes rock, new wave, and smooth jazz.

   Category means:
   a. business
   b. group
   c. success

5. What is your music-listening **style?** Do you listen to music while you do other things, or do you just sit and listen?

   Style means:
   a. a way of doing something
   b. an opinion about something
   c. a type of equipment

6. Music in movies can express many different **emotions.** For example, movie music can sound sad, happy, or scary.

   Emotions means:
   a. feelings
   b. stories
   c. instruments

7. If you want children to **engage with** music, experts say to take them to concerts when they are very young.
   Engage with means:
   a. stay away from
   b. have a career in
   c. be involved with

8. According to music experts, a successful pop song is very simple. **Specifically,** it is easy to remember, and it tells a story that is easy to understand.
   Specifically means:
   a. more exactly
   b. more generally
   c. more closely

9. Music helps some people **concentrate,** but other people find it distracting.
   Concentrate means:
   a. feel relaxed
   b. work harder
   c. pay attention

10. Nigel Kennedy began his career as a classical violinist, but today he plays other **genres,** too. He recorded a jazz album, *SHHH!*, in 2009.
    Genres means:
    a. types
    b. instruments
    c. locations

D COMMUNICATE Work with a partner. Read and answer the questions.

A: *Is there a kind of music that helps you **focus** on your schoolwork?*
B: *Yes. I always listen to jazz when I do homework.*

1. Is there a kind of music that helps you **focus** on your schoolwork? If yes, what kind is it?

2. What other activities do you do while listening to music? What **genres** of music go best with certain activities?

3. What are some of your favorite songs? What **emotions** does each song make you feel?

4. What time of day can you **concentrate** best? What helps you concentrate?

5. For you, what is the most **entertaining** activity to do on a weekend?

6. What are some ways to help children to **engage with** schoolwork?

Nigel Kennedy performs in London.

LISTEN

E 🎧 **1.28** **LISTEN FOR MAIN IDEAS** Listen to the interview. Write each speaker's favorite music genre. Use the genres in the box. There is one extra genre.

> roots music   jazz   folk   rock   classical

Speaker 1   **Speaker 2**   **Speaker 3**   **Speaker 4**

_____   _____   _____   _____

F 🎧 **1.29** **LISTEN FOR DETAILS** Listen to segment 1 of the interview. Complete the statements.

1. Emma heard about a _____. It showed that most people listen to music for more than _____ hours a week.

2. This fact made her wonder: Do people just _____ to music, or do they _____ other things while they're listening?

3. To answer this question, Emma went out on the _____ and interviewed people.

G 🎧 **1.30** **LISTEN FOR DETAILS** Listen to excerpts from the interview. Write the letter of the listening style next to the correct speaker. There is one extra listening style.

Speaker 1 _____   **a.** listens while driving

Speaker 2 _____   **b.** has it on all the time

Speaker 3 _____   **c.** sits in a chair and really listens

Speaker 4 _____   **d.** listens at work

                           e. listens while doing homework

LISTENING SKILL Listen for Reasons

Reasons answer the question *Why*. To identify reasons, listen for words like *because* and *so*. *Because* introduces a reason. *So* follows a reason.

> *I like hip-hop **because** <u>it makes me feel happy.</u>*
>   *reason*

> <u>*I wanted to hear some classical music,*</u> ***so*** *I went to the symphony.*
>   *reason*

H 🎧 **1.31** Listen to excerpts from the interview. Match the reasons with the speaker.

Speakers

Why does Speaker 1 like classical music? _____

Why does Speaker 2 like rock music? _____

Why does Speaker 3 like roots music? _____

Why does Speaker 4 like jazz? _____

Reasons

a. It's relaxing.

b. It helps the speaker focus.

c. It entertains the speaker.

d. The speaker enjoys the emotions it expresses.

AFTER YOU LISTEN

I **THINK CRITICALLY Analyze.** Work with a partner. Discuss your answers to this question:

Do you think there's a connection between someone's personality and the type of music that person likes? For example, do quiet people prefer classical music? Do energetic people prefer rock? Explain your answer.

J Work with a partner. First, read the descriptions of personality types. Check [✓] the one that describes you the best. Tell your partner.

_____ I'm quiet. I like to be still and think.

_____ I have very strong feelings, and I want to change things in life that are not fair.

_____ I'm happy, and I accept life as it is.

_____ I'm very energetic. I'm always doing something.

A girl listens as a man plays the piano on the Marine Parade in Queenstown, New Zealand.

K Take the quiz below. Make sure you understand each music genre. Write the number that shows whether you like each music genre. Then find your personality type.

Music and Personality Quiz

Don't know the genre = 0   Dislike = 1   Like = 2

1 Classical _____

2 Country _____

3 Dance / Electronica _____

4 Folk _____

5 Heavy metal _____

6 Jazz _____

7 Oldies _____

8 Opera _____

9 Pop _____

10 Punk _____

11 Rap / Hip-hop _____

12 Reggae _____

13 Rock _____

14 Movie soundtracks _____

The chart below shows which types of music different personality types tend to prefer. The genres that have the most of your "2"s indicate your personality.

If You Like . . . (Genres),		You . . . (Personality Types)
Classical Jazz Folk Opera		are quiet. You like to be still and think.
Heavy metal Rock Punk		have very strong feelings, and you want to change things in life that are not fair.
Country Pop Oldies Movie soundtracks		are happy, and you accept life as it is.
Dance / Electronica Reggae Rap / Hip-hop		are very energetic. You're always doing something.

Adapted from Rentfrow, P. J., & Gosling, S. D. (2003). The do re mi's of everyday life: The structure and personality correlates of music preferences. *Journal of Personality and Social Psychology, 84*, 1236–1256.

L Work in a small group. Discuss your answers to these questions.

1. Are your quiz results different from the personality type you checked in exercise J?

2. Do you agree with your quiz results? Why, or why not?

3. Have you changed your mind about whether there's a connection between someone's personality and the type of music that person likes? If yes, how?

SPEAKING

SPEAKING SKILL Give Reasons

Speakers often give reasons for their ideas, or reasons for an event or happening. If your reasons are clear, your listeners will be more likely to understand your ideas.

Earlier you listened to speakers use words like *so* and *because* to give reasons.

Here are some other expressions to signal reasons:

Expressions	Reasons
The reason that	*I like to stream music is that it's easy.*
One reason that	*I like to go to concerts is that the music sounds better.*
The main reason that	*I buy music is to support the musicians.*

(See page 169 of the *Independent Student Handbook* for more expressions used to signal reasons.)

M THINK CRITICALLY Personalize. In the chart below, list songs, performers, or music genres that you like. Write a reason that you like each one. Then talk to a partner about your opinions. Use the words and expressions for giving reasons.

A: *I like hip-hop. The reason that I like it is that it makes me want to dance. What kind of music do you like?*

B: *I like classical. One reason that I like it is that it helps me to concentrate.*

Songs, Performers, or Music Genres	Reasons
hip-hop	It makes me want to dance.

PRONUNCIATION SKILL   Contractions with *Be*

In speaking, we often combine the verb *be* with the subject pronoun. The combined words are called *contractions*. Although it is important to know what two words are combined in a contraction, you should pronounce a contraction like one word.

🎧 **1.32**

what is ⟶ what's   who is ⟶ who's

we are ⟶ we're   he is ⟶ he's

it is ⟶ it's   there are ⟶ there're

she is ⟶ she's   they are ⟶ they're

Note: *They're* and *there're* have similar sounds. To know the difference, pay attention to the way speakers use them in sentences.

N 🎧 **1.33** Listen to the speaker. Choose the sentence you hear.

1. a. There are a lot of good soundtracks.   b. There're a lot of good soundtracks.

2. a. It is my favorite song.   b. It's my favorite song.

3. a. Who is your favorite composer?   b. Who's your favorite composer?

4. a. She is a famous songwriter.   b. She's a famous songwriter.

5. a. They are going to a concert.   b. They're going to a concert.

6. a. He is a very good guitar player.   b. He's a very good guitar player.

O Practice pronouncing contractions. First, underline the contractions in these sentences from the interview. Then read the sentences aloud to a partner.

1. Today, we're talking about music.

2. There's music all around us.

3. That's a lot of listening!

4. Do they do other things while they're listening?

5. It's a big category.

6. What's your music listening style?

"Wolfman" Washington singing the blues at the New Orleans Jazz Festival 2013

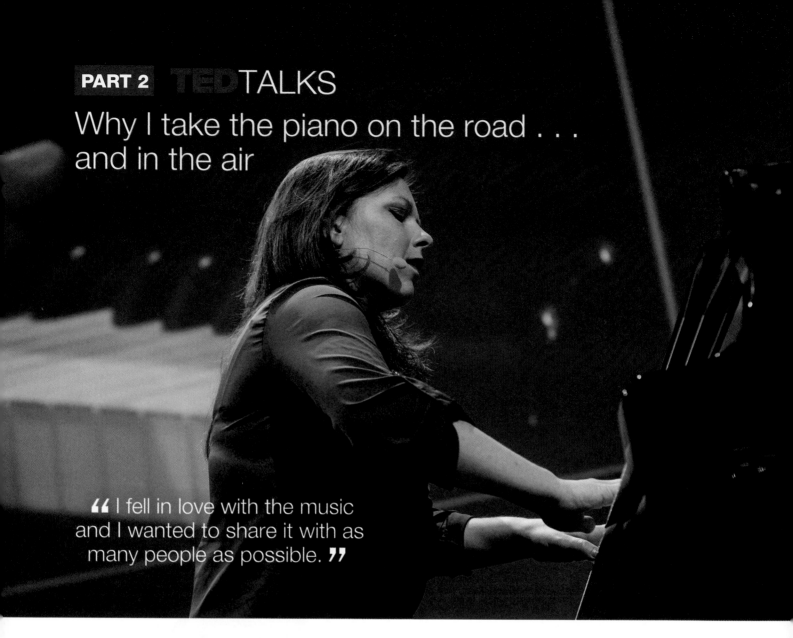

Why I take the piano on the road . . . and in the air

❝ I fell in love with the music and I wanted to share it with as many people as possible. **❞**

BEFORE YOU WATCH

A THINK CRITICALLY Predict. Read the title and information about the TED speaker. What do you think she will talk about?

> **DARIA VAN DEN BERCKEN** Pianist
>
> Daria van den Bercken loves classical music, and she wants the world to love it, too.
>
> The Dutch / Russian pianist plays with several orchestras in the Netherlands, but she plays music in some unusual places, too, such as in the air and driving down streets. Because of her enthusiasm and her unusual performances, Daria attracts many new listeners to her favorite music, including very young children.
>
> Daria van den Bercken's idea worth spreading is that we should try to enjoy music the way a child does—full of wonder and with pure amazement.

B COMMUNICATE Work with a partner. Discuss these questions.

> A: *Do you like classical music?*
>
> B: *Yes, I do. It's relaxing.*

1. Western classical music usually refers to music that was written in Europe or North America from the 17th century to the present day. Beethoven and Mozart are examples of classical composers. Do you like classical music? Why, or why not?

2. What do you associate with classical music? That is, how does it make you feel, or what does it make you think about?

VOCABULARY

C 🎧 **1.34** The sentences below will help you learn words in the TED Talk. Read and listen to the sentences. Guess the meanings of the words and phrases in bold. Then write each word and phrase next to its definition on page 74.

a. Beethoven was a classical **composer**. He wrote symphonies and other works of music during the late 18th century and the early 19th century.

b. Daria van den Bercken believes that young children listen to classical music without **prejudice** because they are too young to have any ideas about it yet.

c. One way to **reach** students who are having trouble understanding a concept is to relate the concept to their everyday lives.

d. Some people are good at playing the piano. I can't **relate to** that because I'm not very musical.

e. Some people don't like jazz music because of its **complexity**. They prefer simpler musical genres such as pop music.

f. Happiness and sadness are **contrasting** emotions. They are opposites.

g. Jazz is a **constant** part of my life. I listen to it all day long.

h. Some rock music is very **energetic**. It sounds very active, and it makes me want to get up and move around.

i. The music of the French composer Debussy sounds dreamy and **magical** to me. It has a very charming, enchanting sound.

j. The **elements** of pop music include repetition—repeating sounds—and hooks, which are sounds or words that make listeners pay attention.

1. _____constant_____ (adj) happening all the time

2. _____ (n) parts

3. _____ (n) a person who writes music

4. _____ (adj) having energy; active

5. _____ (v) understand

6. _____ (adj) having a wonderful or delightful quality

7. _____ (v) connect with

8. _____ (n) an opinion based on general dislike or good feelings, rather than facts or reasons

9. _____ (adj) showing a difference

10. _____ (n) the condition of having many difficult parts

D **COMMUNICATE** Read the statements. Write A if you agree and D if you disagree. Then discuss your answers with a partner.

> A: *I disagree with number one. I feel most **energetic** in the evening.*
>
> B: *Why?*
>
> A: *I'm a night person.*

1. _____ I feel most **energetic** in the morning.

2. _____ I find it easy to **relate to** young children.

3. _____ Social media is a **constant** part of my life.

4. _____ My friends and I often have **contrasting** opinions about things like movies, books, and music.

5. _____ The best way to **reach** my friends is by email.

6. _____ Everyone has some **prejudice.**

7. _____ Only children have **magical** moments.

8. _____ The most important **element** of learning English is vocabulary.

WATCH

learn**more** George Friedrich Handel was born in Germany in 1685 but spent most of his adult life in London. He wrote music for singers and choirs, including operas. He is also well known for his organ music. Handel also wrote keyboard* music, but the keyboard music of other composers at the time was much more famous.

*To Handel, a "keyboard" was a harpsichord, an early type of piano.

E ▶ **1.19 WATCH FOR MAIN IDEAS** Watch the TED Talk. Check [✓] the two statements that you think van den Bercken would agree with.

1. _____ If you love something, you should try to share it with other people.

2. _____ Older children can deal with the complexity of classical music better than younger children can.

3. _____ Everyone should listen to music the way young children do.

4. _____ All music expresses contrasting emotions.

F **THINK CRITICALLY Reflect.** Work with a partner. Compare your answers to exercise E. Which statements do you agree with? Which statements do you disagree with? Explain your answers.

NOTE-TAKING SKILL **Write Key Words or Short Sentences**

You don't have to write complete sentences when you take notes. It's quicker to write key words, phrases, or short sentences. Leave out small words like *the* and *of*. Focus on nouns, verbs, names, and numbers. It doesn't matter if words are missing as long as you understand what your phrases or short sentences mean.

　　Complete sentence: *Van den Bercken fell in love with the music of Handel.*
　　Key words / phrase: *loves Handel*

Note: Leave out names that are repeated. For example, we know this talk is about van den Bercken's experiences. We don't have to repeat her name.

WORDS IN THE TALK
browsing (v): (in computers) going from place to place on the World Wide Web without a clear goal
melancholic (adj): giving the feeling of deep sadness
the media (n): television, radio, news magazines, newspapers, and the Internet

G ▶ **1.20** **WATCH FOR DETAILS** Watch each segment of the TED Talk. Listen for answers to the questions. Write the answers using key words or short sentences.

Segment 1

1. In what country did van den Bercken play Handel while flying?

_____

2. In what city did she play Handel while driving down streets?

_____

3. Van den Bercken was especially amazed by one type of Handel's music. What was it, and why did she like it so much?

_____

4. Where did she find this music?

_____

5. How does her onstage performance of Handel sound at first? How does the music change?

_____

Segment 2

1. According to van den Bercken, how do children who are 7–8 years old listen to music?

_____

2. Why does she think older children might not like classical music?

_____

H **CHECK YOUR NOTES** With a partner, compare your answers from exercise G. Can you understand your own notes? Ask your partner questions about any answers that you are not sure about.

    A: *What did you write for number 1?*

    B: *I wrote "played Handel flying Brazil." What did you write?*

I ▶ **1.21** **WATCH FOR REASONS** Listen to an excerpt from the TED Talk. Then discuss with a partner your answer to this question: Why did van den Bercken play Handel in the air and while driving down the street?

J ▶ **1.22** **EXPAND YOUR VOCABULARY** Watch the excerpts from the TED Talk. Guess the meanings of the phrases in the box.

> day-to-day   being in awe of   are open to   state of wonder

AFTER YOU WATCH

K COMMUNICATE Work with a partner. Discuss your answers to these questions.

1. What are some ways to get friends or family members to appreciate something that you really like, such as a book, a movie, or a type of music?

2. How have your musical tastes changed as you've grown up?

Van den Bercken playing piano in Brazil

L THINK CRITICALLY Interpret an Infographic. Work with a partner. Study the infographic. It shows how people answered the question: How much time do you spend each week listening to music in these situations? Read the statements about the infographic below and write T for *true* and F for *false*. Then correct the false statements.

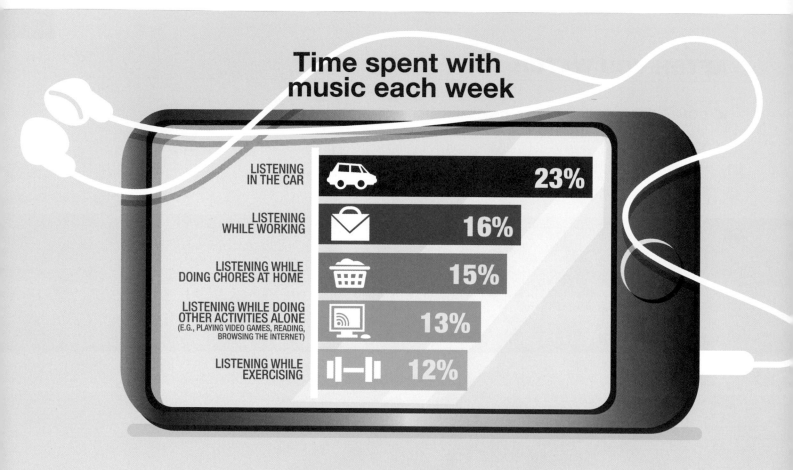

Time spent with music each week

LISTENING IN THE CAR	🚗	**23%**
LISTENING WHILE WORKING	🛍	**16%**
LISTENING WHILE DOING CHORES AT HOME	🧺	**15%**
LISTENING WHILE DOING OTHER ACTIVITIES ALONE (E.G., PLAYING VIDEO GAMES, READING, BROWSING THE INTERNET)	📺	**13%**
LISTENING WHILE EXERCISING	🏋	**12%**

1. _____ Of the time people spend listening to music each week, they are in a car 13 percent of the time.

2. _____ The greatest proportion of time spent with music occurs while people are working.

3. _____ People spend more time listening to music while they work than they do while doing chores at home.

4. _____ The smallest proportion of time spent with music occurs when people are exercising.

5. _____ People spend 15 percent of all weekly listening time doing activities such as playing video games or reading.

M COMMUNICATE Work with a partner. Compare your answers to exercise L. Then discuss your answers to these questions: Which activities do you do the most while listening to music? The least?

Put It Together

A **THINK CRITICALLY Synthesize.** Work in a small group. In what ways are the people in the interview in Part 1 and Daria van den Bercken similar or different? Complete the Venn diagram with the correct letters.

a. listens to music to help concentrate on work

b. feels energized by music

c. plays an instrument

d. listens to only one type of music

e. listens to music to feel strong emotions

f. gives concerts for children

g. listens to or plays music while moving / traveling

h. is a professional musician

i. listens to music to learn about the people who created it

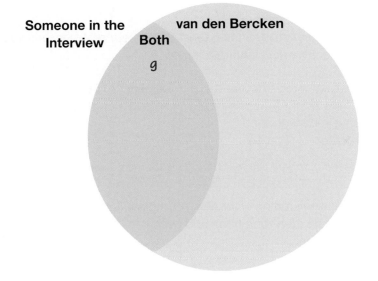

Someone in the Interview   Both   van den Bercken

g

B Compare your Venn diagram in exercise A with another group's. Explain your answers.

COMMUNICATE

ASSIGNMENT: Give an Individual Presentation You will give an individual presentation to a group about your music listening style. Review the ideas in Parts 1 and 2 and the listening and speaking skills as you prepare your presentation.

PREPARE

PRESENTATION SKILL Use an Effective Hook

A good presentation begins with a hook. A hook is something that gets the audience's attention. Here are some types of hooks:

- an interesting quote
- a surprising fact
- an anecdote (a short story)

Hooks should be related to the topic of your presentation. Here are some examples of hooks related to music:

Quote: *As the rock musician Bono once said, "Music can change the world because it can change people."*

Surprising fact: *A recent study showed that 93 percent of Americans spend more than 25 hours a week listening to music.*

▶ **1.23** Watch the beginning of Daria van den Bercken's TED Talk. For her hook, she uses an anecdote about how she flew over a crowd of thousands of people in Brazil playing music by Handel.

(See page 177 in the *Independent Student Handbook* for more examples of effective hooks.)

C Think about your music listening style. First, complete items 2–5 in the presentation outline. Then think of an idea for a hook and write it in the outline. Finally, discuss your outline with a partner.

1. Idea for a hook: _____

2. My favorite music genre / What I listen to the most: _____

3. Why this is my favorite / Why I listen to this genre the most: _____

_____

4. When I listen / What I'm doing when I listen: _____

_____

5. Why I listen this way (how it makes me feel, helps me do something, and so on):

_____

_____

D **COLLABORATE** Work with a partner. Practice your presentation. Use your outline. As you practice,

- use words and expressions for giving reasons.
- remember to pronounce contractions with *be* correctly.

E Read the rubric on page 181 before you present. Notice how your presentation will be evaluated. Keep these categories in mind as you present and watch your classmates' presentations.

PRESENT

F Give your presentation to a small group. Watch your classmates' presentations. After you watch each one, provide feedback using the rubric as a guide. Add notes and any other feedback you want to share.

G **THINK CRITICALLY** **Evaluate.** In a small group, discuss the feedback you received. Discuss what you did well and what might make your presentation even stronger.

REFLECT

Reflect on what you have learned. Check [✓] your progress.

I can
- ☐ listen for reasons.
- ☐ give reasons.
- ☐ understand contractions with *be*.
- ☐ take notes using key words or short sentences.
- ☐ start a presentation with an effective hook.

I understand the meanings of these words and can use them.
Circle those you know. Underline those you need to work on.

category AWL	contrasting AWL	entertaining	reach
complexity AWL	element AWL	focus AWL	relate to
composer	emotion	genre	specifically AWL
concentrate AWL	energetic AWL	magical	style AWL
constant AWL	engage with	prejudice	transport AWL

Give Thanks

School teacher Sakhalin Finnie receives the Milken National Educator Award and the gratitude of her students at Harbor Teacher Preparation Academy, California.

THINK AND DISCUSS

1 Read the unit title. What does it mean?

2 Look at the photo and read the caption. How do you think Sakhalin Finnie feels? How do you think the people in the audience feel? Why do you think Finnie received the award?

The Power of Gratitude

BEFORE YOU LISTEN

A COMMUNICATE Work in a small group. Discuss these questions.

1. Look at the photo and read the caption. What are you thankful for?

2. Who do you often say "thank you" to? What do you thank people for?

3. When did someone recently say "thank you" to you? Why did the person say it? How did you feel when the person said it?

B THINK CRITICALLY Predict. You are going to hear a presentation called *The Power of Gratitude*. If a thing or a person has *power*, they have a special ability. *Gratitude* means thankfulness. In what ways do you think gratitude can be powerful? Discuss your ideas with your group.

Boys say *Namaste*, "Thank you," at a school near Manali in Northern India.

VOCABULARY

C 🎧 **2.2** Read and listen to the sentences with words from the presentation. Guess the meaning of each bold word or phrase. Then write each word or phrase next to its definition.

a. Grateful people are **aware of** the good things in their lives. They pay attention to these things, and they know how important they are.

b. People who are thankful often have a positive **attitude**. They feel good about life.

c. I am **grateful** for everything you have done for me. Thank you.

d. **Stress** can make you sick. It's better for your health to feel relaxed.

e. People often get more work done if someone appreciates them. For example, workers are often more **productive** when their bosses say "thank you."

f. When you see a kind act, say "thank you." **Recognizing** kindness makes people happy.

g. Gratitude can change people's feelings. It can **affect** them in a good way.

h. **Researchers** such as psychologists study human behavior. They are interested in how our thinking is related to our behavior.

i. When I work hard, no one **acknowledges** it. I wish someone would notice my work.

j. When a person **expresses** thanks, they usually say "thank you."

1. _____affect_____ (v) change

2. _____ (adj) knowledgeable about; have an understanding of

3. _____ (v) accepts that something exists or happened

4. _____ (v) says

5. _____ (adj) thankful

6. _____ (v) noticing

7. _____ (adj) able to accomplish a lot

8. _____ (n) a feeling about someone or something

9. _____ (n) mental or physical difficulty caused by pressure

10. _____ (n) people who study something deeply

D COMMUNICATE Work with a partner. Take turns asking and answering the questions. Use the words in bold in your answers.

> A: *Do you have a positive **attitude** about life?*
>
> B: *Yes. I have a very positive **attitude**. I always think that good things are going to happen to me. How about you?*

1. Do you have a positive **attitude** about life? Give an example.

2. What time of day are you the most **productive**? Why is this your most productive time?

3. Does stress **affect** you? If yes, how? If no, why not?

4. What are some of the positive things in your life that you are **aware of**?

5. How do you feel when you do something nice and someone **acknowledges** it?

LISTEN

E 🎧 **2.3** ▶ **1.24** **LISTEN FOR MAIN IDEAS** Read the statements. Then listen to the presentation. What is it mainly about? Choose the answer that best completes the statement.

The presentation is about _____.

a. ways to become more grateful

b. the benefits of being grateful

c. how gratitude can help you at work

d. how gratitude improves friendship

LISTENING SKILL Listen for Key Words and Phrases

The main ideas of a presentation are the most important ideas. Speakers usually repeat key words and phrases to highlight the main ideas. They also use synonyms (words with the same meaning) of key words and phrases to stress the main ideas. Listen for key words and synonyms to get the main ideas.

🎧 **2.4** ***People who have an "attitude of gratitude"*** *have good physical health.*
        key phrase

Grateful people *have better mental health, too.*
        synonym

F 🎧 **2.3** In the presentation, the speaker talks about gratitude. She uses the word *gratitude* and synonyms of it. Listen to the presentation again. Check [✓] the key words and phrases every time you hear them. Which ones does the speaker use the most?

_____ gratitude   _____ grateful (people)

_____ gratefulness   _____ being grateful

_____ thankfulness   _____ appreciation

NOTE-TAKING SKILL   **Use a Mind Map**

A graphic organizer is a visual way to organize your notes. One kind of graphic organizer is a mind map. A mind map shows connections between ideas. The mind map below connects main ideas and details.

G 🎧 **2.5** **LISTEN FOR DETAILS** Listen to segment 1 of the presentation. Think about how gratitude affects mental and physical health. Complete the mind map with the letters of the correct phrases from the box.

> **a.** sleep better   **d.** take better care of themselves
>
> **b.** have less stress   **e.** have better health
>
> **c.** are happier   **f.** have better social relationships

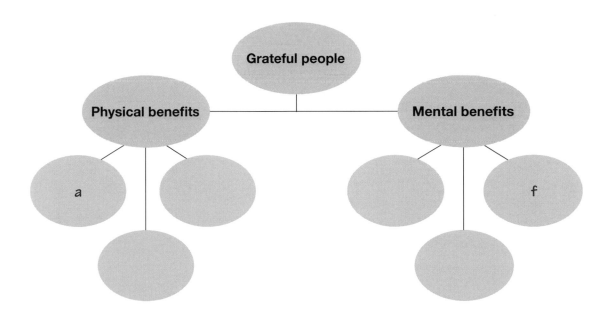

H 🎧 **2.6 LISTEN FOR DETAILS** Listen to segment 2 of the presentation. Think about how gratitude affects companies and workers. Match the causes and the effects.

CAUSES	EFFECTS
1. People receive gratitude at work. ⟶ _____	a. They become more helpful.
2. Mattel recognizes and praises employees. ⟶ _____	b. They become more productive.
3. In a study, people receive thanks. ⟶ _____	c. The company gets on a "best company to work for" list.

I 🎧 **2.7 LISTEN FOR DETAILS** Listen to segment 3 of the presentation. Complete the tips for becoming more grateful. Use the words and phrases from the box. There are two extra words.

> actions   notice   express   write down   please   thank you

1. Each day, _____ things that you are thankful for.

2. Say "_____" more often.

3. Try to _____ when other people do kind acts.

4. Thank people for their kind _____.

AFTER YOU LISTEN

J **THINK CRITICALLY** **Analyze.** Work with a partner. Answer these questions. Use the information from the presentation to support your answers.

1. Does the presenter believe that you can become a grateful person? How do you know?

2. Do you think grateful people are more successful? Why, or why not?

K **THINK CRITICALLY Personalize.** Are you a grateful person? Take the quiz to find out. For each statement, choose the answer that describes you. Then add up your score: Never =1 point; Sometimes = 2 points; Often = 3 points.

How grateful are you?

1 I feel very thankful for my physical health.

    1. Never   2. Sometimes   3. Often

2 I feel happy about my life.

    1. Never   2. Sometimes   3. Often

3 I feel thankful for my friends.

    1. Never   2. Sometimes   3. Often

4 I feel thankful for my family.

    1. Never   2. Sometimes   3. Often

5 I tell my friends how much I appreciate them.

    1. Never   2. Sometimes   3. Often

6 I tell family members how much I appreciate them.

    1. Never   2. Sometimes   3. Often

7 I feel glad that I have basic things in life like food, clothing, and shelter.

    1. Never   2. Sometimes   3. Often

8 Even on a bad day, I realize that I still have many good things in my life.

    1. Never   2. Sometimes   3. Often

L **COMMUNICATE** Work in a small group. Discuss these questions.

1. The higher your score is, the more grateful you probably are. What was your score? Were you surprised by the results? Why, or why not?

2. Do you want to become a more grateful person? If so, what can you do to become more grateful?

SPEAKING

SPEAKING SKILL Support Ideas with Examples

Examples make ideas clearer and more interesting. They help listeners understand the speaker's key points. Speakers often introduce a main idea and then give examples.

Speakers often use signals to introduce examples, but not always. The most common signal is *for example*. Look at these examples from the presentation:

With a signal:

*Grateful people have better mental health, too. **For example**, they have less stress.*
          main idea   example

Without a signal:

They're finding that grateful people have better physical health. They get sick less
                                     main idea

often and see a doctor less often.
          example

M 🎧 **2.8 COLLABORATE** Work with a partner. Read and listen to these excerpts from the presentation. Underline examples of the following:

- the meaning of gratitude
- how gratitude affects people who receive it

1. "So, what do you think I mean by gratitude? [. . .] It's a feeling of thankfulness, a feeling of appreciation. It's being aware of the good things in your life, appreciating small things, counting your blessings. Some psychologists call this an 'attitude of gratitude.'"

2. "Gratitude can affect the person who receives thanks, too. For example, it can make them more helpful. In one study, people gave a student some help. The student thanked some of the people. He did not thank other people in the study. Then the student asked for more help. The people he thanked gave more help. The people he did not thank gave less help."

N **COMMUNICATE** As a class, discuss the answers to these questions about the excerpts in exercise M.

1. What are three examples of gratitude?

2. How does the speaker explain that gratitude can affect the person who receives thanks?

PRONUNCIATION Sentence Stress

In English, speakers normally *stress* words that give important, and often new, information in a sentence. Stressed words are higher, louder, and more clearly pronounced than unstressed words. This makes it easier to hear them.

Words That Are Normally Stressed*	Words That Are Normally Unstressed
nouns, verbs, adjectives	articles
negatives	prepositions
(*Wh-*) question words	pronouns
numbers	auxiliary verbs (*do, have, should, will*, etc.)
adverbs	the verb *be*

2.9 Read and listen to these sentences. Notice how the bold words are stressed.

*Today, we're going to be discussing **gratitude**.*

*We're going to talk about the **power** of gratitude.*

*These are general rules. A speaker can choose to stress any word that he or she thinks is important.

O **2.10** Listen and underline the stressed words.

1. So, what do you think I mean by gratitude?

2. It's a feeling of thankfulness, a feeling of appreciation.

3. They're finding that grateful people have better physical health.

4. Grateful people have better mental health, too.

5. Gratitude is important at work as well.

6. Gratitude can affect the person who receives thanks, too.

P **2.10** Listen again. Repeat the sentences. Make sure the stressed words are higher, louder, and more clearly pronounced than the unstressed words.

Q **COMMUNICATE** Work with a partner. Read the questions silently. Underline the stressed words. Then take turns asking and answering the questions. Give examples in your answers and pay attention to sentence stress.

A: *Who is the **happiest** person you know?*

B: *My **brother**. He has a lot of **friends** and he **laughs** a lot.*

1. Who is the happiest person you know? Why do you think he or she is happy?

2. Are you a productive person? What are some ways to be more productive?

3. What are some ways to acknowledge someone who helps you, such as a teacher?

Why lunch ladies are heroes

" A *thank you* can change a life. **"**

BEFORE YOU WATCH

A **THINK CRITICALLY** **Predict.** Read the title and information about the TED speaker. Think of some examples of heroes. Then answer this question: What do you think this talk will be about? Tell your class.

JARRETT J. KROSOCZKA Author and Illustrator

Jarrett J. Krosoczka is a lifelong storyteller. He wrote his first book at the age of eight. While he was a college student at Rhode Island School of Design, he started drawing pictures for children's books. He got his first book contract six months after he graduated. Krosoczka is the author of 18 picture books for children, and he's still writing books. His *Lunch Lady* book series is being made into a movie. In addition, Krosoczka has a radio show about books for children.

Jarrett J. Krosoczka's idea worth spreading is that a simple *thank you* can change the life of the giver and the receiver.

B Think about your answers to the following questions.

1. Where did you eat lunch when you were a child in school? Who prepared your lunch?

2. Did you have people who served lunch at your school? If so, what do you remember about them?

3. What other kinds of workers help out at schools? Why are their jobs important?

C COMMUNICATE Work with a partner. Discuss your answers from exercise B.

A: *I ate lunch at school, but I don't remember the cafeteria workers very well. Did you have cafeteria workers at your school?*

B: *Yes, I did. Everyone liked them. They were really friendly and helpful.*

learn**more** A *lunch lady* is a woman who prepares and serves lunch to schoolchildren. As in other countries, there is a school lunch program in the United States. It provides free or low-cost lunches in over 100,000 schools.

Lunch ladies prepare and serve food in a *cafeteria*, a place to eat in a school. In the TED Talk, the speaker also talks about a *cafetorium*. *Cafetorium* is a combination of the words *cafeteria* and *auditorium*. Some schools use one room, a cafetorium, for both purposes.

VOCABULARY

D 🎧 **2.11** The sentences below will help you learn words in the TED Talk. Read and listen to the sentences. Guess the meaning of each bold word or phrase. Then complete each question with the correct word or phrase.

a. I **attended** a public school. I didn't go to a private school.

b. Krosoczka used his **imagination** to write. He used his original ideas to write many popular children's books.

c. Meeting his lunch lady **inspired** Krosoczka. It gave him the idea to write children's books about a lunch lady hero.

d. Krosoczka wanted to acknowledge lunch ladies for their hard work, so he decided to **create** "School Lunch Hero Day."

e. Krosoczka had an **encounter** with his lunch lady years after he graduated. He didn't expect to meet her, but the meeting changed his life.

f. School lunch **programs** in the United States feed more than 31 million children. The plan to feed children at school started in the 1940s.

g. The lunch ladies at my school **treated** the children well. They behaved in a kind and friendly way.

h. Krosoczka explains how many students at a school in Kentucky **rely on** meals that lunch ladies prepare because they don't get enough food at home.

i. My teacher cried when we thanked him at the end of the school year. We were surprised by his **response**.

j. If you **participate** in class, you will do better in school. Being involved in class activities is the best way to learn.

1. Do you usually _____ in your English class? What are some good reasons to be involved in class activities?

2. Do you have a good _____? If so, how do you use it? Do your original ideas help you in school? Do you use them for your hobbies?

3. If you say "thank you" in your native language, what is the usual _____? What does the other person say to you?

4. Do you have _____ in your community that help certain groups of people, such as children or senior citizens? If so, how do these plans help people?

5. Should your community _____ organizations in order to help people? Who should put these organizations together?

6. If you _____ a public school, did you like it? Did you want to go to a private school instead? If you went to a private school, did you like it? Did you want to go to a public school instead?

7. Can you think of a time when a teacher or classmate _____ you in a kind way? What did he or she do or say? How did you feel?

8. Think of an event in the past that _____ you, like Krosoczka's meeting with his lunch lady. How did the event change your life?

9. When was the last time you had an _____ with an old friend? What did you talk about when you met this person?

10. Of all your friends, who do you _____ most? Why is this friend the best person to depend on?

E **COMMUNICATE** Work in a small group. Take turns asking and answering the questions in exercise D.

WATCH

F ▶ **1.25** **WATCH FOR MAIN IDEAS** Watch the TED Talk. Check [✓] the four statements that Krosoczka might agree with.

1. _____ Lunch ladies do more than just make lunch.

2. _____ Anyone can be a superhero.

3. _____ People usually treat lunch ladies very kindly.

4. _____ When children acknowledge their lunch ladies, it can have very positive effects.

5. _____ Lunch ladies are important people in the lives of children.

G **THINK CRITICALLY Reflect.** Work with a partner. Discuss your answers to these questions.

1. In your opinion, who are some other school workers that are also "superheroes" (like lunch ladies)?

2. Were there any "superhero" school workers at your school? What did they do? How did they help you or other students?

WORDS IN THE TALK
guidance counselor (n): a person who helps children with problems or helps them plan their education

H ▶ **1.26 WATCH FOR DETAILS** Watch each segment of the TED Talk. Complete the sentences. Use the words from the boxes.

Segment 1 The *Lunch Lady* Book Series

> fish   idea   monsters   school   served

1. One day, Krosoczka saw his lunch lady at his old

   _____ .

2. Seeing her gave him the _____ for the
   Lunch Lady series.

3. The lunch ladies' nunchucks (a kind of weapon) are made
   from _____ sticks.

4. Krosoczka's lunch ladies fight _____ with
   nunchucks.

5. When the lunch ladies get the bad guy, they say, "Justice is

   _____ !"

Segment 2 The Effects of the Series

> kids   lunch ladies   recognize

1. The *Lunch Lady* books had an effect on _____ .
   They wrote letters and made artwork.

2. The *Lunch Lady* books had an effect on _____ .
   They felt acknowledged.

3. As a result, Krosoczka started School Lunch Hero Day. On this day,

   kids _____ lunch ladies.

Segment 3 *Lunch Lady* Heroes

> food   problems   serve

1. Lunch ladies do more than cook and _____ food.

2. Some lunch ladies help children with _____ .

3. Some lunch ladies feed kids who don't get enough _____ .

Segment 4 The Power of "Thank You"

> changes   expresses   important

1. Of course lunch ladies are _____. They provide children with food, and children can't learn if they're hungry.

2. Gratefulness _____ peoples' lives.

3. It affects the person who receives it and the person who _____ it.

I ▶ **1.27 GIVE EXAMPLES** Watch segment 3 again. Listen for examples. Complete the mind map with the letters of the examples.

> **a.** made their own *Lunch Lady* comics
>
> **b.** talked to the guidance counselor
>
> **c.** traveled in a bus to feed children in the summer
>
> **d.** made milk carton flower vases

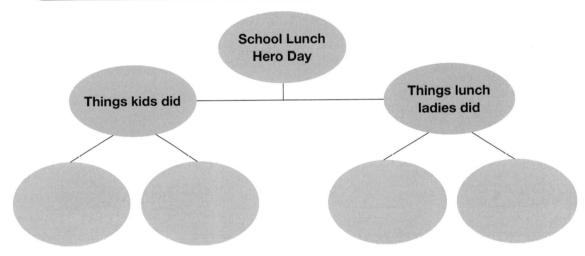

J ▶ **1.28 EXPAND YOUR VOCABULARY** Watch the excerpts from the TED Talk. Guess the meanings of the phrases in the box.

> blew my mind   was moved by   keep a close eye on   passed away

AFTER YOU WATCH

K THINK CRITICALLY Analyze. Work with a partner. Discuss your answers to these questions.

1. In his graphic novels, who does Krosoczka compare a lunch lady with? Why does the audience laugh at this?

2. Krosoczka tells the audience what a lunch lady said about School Lunch Hero Day, "Before this day, I felt like I was at the end of the planet at this school. I didn't think that anyone noticed us down here." Why did the lunch lady think that no one noticed them before this day?

L THINK CRITICALLY Interpret an Infographic. Work with a partner. Study the infographic. Then complete the sentences about it. Use the words from the box.

7 percent	7 years	10 percent	20 percent
benefits	Denmark	feelings	South Africa

1. The purpose of the infographic is to show some

   _____ of gratitude.

2. Grateful people give _____ more time and money

   to charities (organizations that help people).

3. Grateful people have _____ fewer illnesses that

   are related to stress.

4. The incomes of happy people are _____ higher.

5. _____ is a more grateful country than

   _____ .

6. People who have positive _____ can live

   _____ longer.

What good is gratitude?

Charity
Grateful people on average give 20% more time & money

Psychology
Gratitude is related to age: For every 10 years, gratitude increases by 5%

Community
Grateful people will have a stronger bond with the local community

Health
Grateful people will have 10% fewer stress-related illnesses, be more physically fit, and have blood pressure that is lower by 12%

Work
Happy people's income is roughly 7% higher

Friends
Grateful people will have more satisfying relationships with others, and will be better liked

Youth
Grateful youth have 13% fewer fights and are 20% more likely to get A grades

Where
The most grateful countries are South Africa, UAE, Philippines, & India
Least: Netherlands, Denmark, Hungary, Czech Republic, & UK

Life
Overall positive emotions can add up to 7 years to your life

Put It Together

A THINK CRITICALLY Synthesize. Work in a small group. Complete the chart with information from the presentation in Part 1 and the TED Talk in Part 2. There is more than one possible answer for some blanks.

QUESTIONS	PRESENTATION: THE POWER OF GRATITUDE	TED TALK: WHY LUNCH LADIES ARE HEROES
1. What are some ways to show gratitude?	• say _____ more often • thank people around you who _____	• say _____ to lunch ladies • children became very creative: they made _____ for their lunch ladies
2. How does gratitude affect people who give thanks?	• have better physical _____ • have better _____ health	• According to Krosoczka, gratitude changes _____ of the person who expresses it.
3. How does gratitude affect people who receive thanks?	• In a study, people became more _____ when a student thanked them. • It feels _____ to help. • When you feel good, you want to be even more _____.	• School Lunch Hero Day made one lunch lady feel _____.

B THINK CRITICALLY Personalize. Think of examples of how the ideas from the presentation and from the TED Talk apply to your own life. Discuss your ideas with a partner.

COMMUNICATE

ASSIGNMENT: Give an Individual Presentation You will give an individual presentation about a time when giving or receiving gratitude affected you or someone you know. Review the ideas in Parts 1 and 2 and the listening and speaking skills as you prepare your presentation.

PREPARE

PRESENTATION SKILL Tell a Personal Story

Telling a personal story is a powerful way to illustrate your message. When you include a personal story, the audience understands how you feel about a subject and why it's important to you.

When you tell a story, make sure it

- relates to your topic/supports your message.
- is interesting.
- is easy to follow.

C Think of a time in your life when giving or receiving gratitude affected you or someone you know. Write notes on the main parts of your personal story. Then share your notes with a partner. Ask and answer questions about your notes. Make sure your ideas are clear and well organized.

> **My Personal Story**
>
> When did the event take place? _____
>
> Where did the event take place? _____
>
> Who were the people involved? (Describe them.) _____
>
> What happened first? _____
>
> What happened next? _____
>
> How does your story end? _____
>
> What did you learn? OR: What can the audience learn from your story? _____
>
> _____

D **COLLABORATE** Work with a partner. Practice your presentation. Use your notes. As you practice:

- Use key words and phrases to introduce your main points.
- Use *for example* to introduce your examples.

E Read the rubric on page 182 before you present. Notice how your presentation will be evaluated. Keep these categories in mind as you present and watch your classmates' presentations.

PRESENT

F Give your presentation to a small group. Watch your classmates' presentations. After you watch each one, provide feedback using the rubric as a guide. Add notes and any other feedback you want to share.

G **THINK CRITICALLY Evaluate.** In a small group, discuss the feedback you received. Discuss what you did well and what might make your presentation even stronger.

REFLECT

Reflect on what you have learned. Check [✓] your progress.

I can
- ☐ listen for key words and phrases.
- ☐ use a mind map.
- ☐ support ideas with examples.
- ☐ stress key words in a sentence.
- ☐ tell a personal story.

I understand the meanings of these words and phrases and can use them.
Circle those you know. Underline those you need to work on.

acknowledge AWL	aware of AWL	grateful	productive	researcher AWL
affect AWL	create AWL	imagination	program	response AWL
attend	encounter AWL	inspire	recognize	stress AWL
attitude AWL	express	participate AWL	rely on AWL	treat

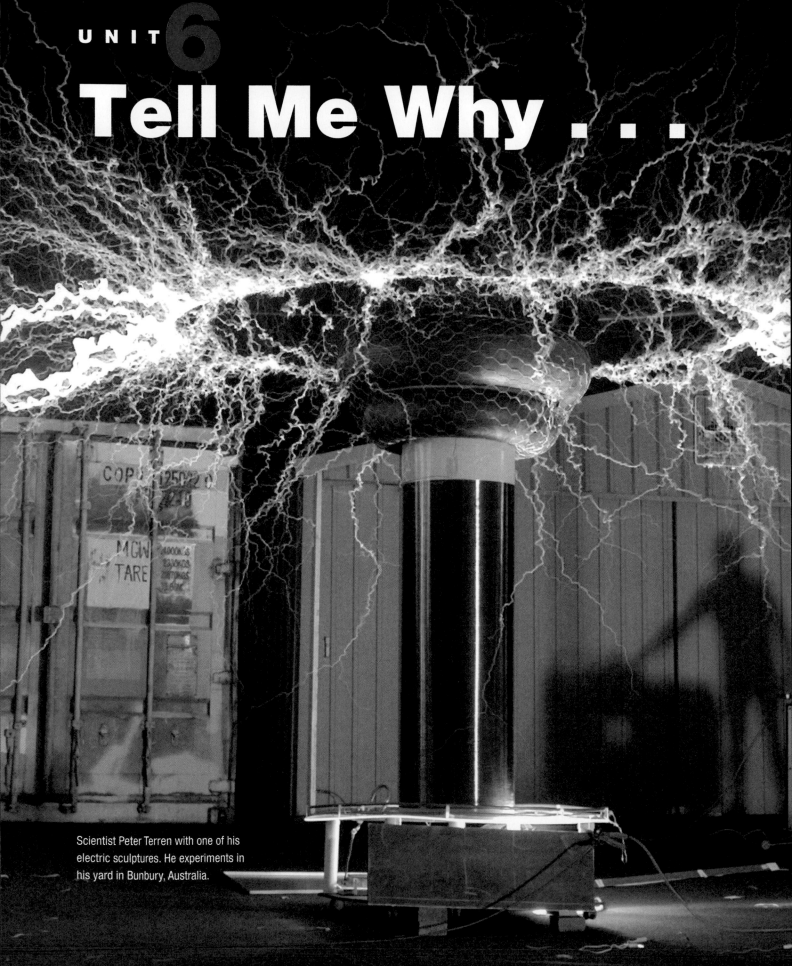

Tell Me Why . . .

Scientist Peter Terren with one of his
electric sculptures. He experiments in
his yard in Bunbury, Australia.

THINK AND DISCUSS

1 Read the unit title. What do you think it means? Who usually asks this question?

2 Look at the photo and read the caption. Why do you think Terren makes electric sculptures? Is this something you want to do?

BEFORE YOU LISTEN

A COMMUNICATE Work in a small group. Discuss these questions.

1. Look at the photo and read the caption. What is the child doing? Why? Did you do an "experiment" like this when you were a child?

2. What does *curious* mean? Is curiosity a good thing? Give examples of how curiosity can have benefits.

B 🎧 **2.12 THINK CRITICALLY Predict.** You are going to hear three students talking about curiosity. Listen to the first part of the conversation. What is Juan's question? How does Nancy answer? Can you guess how David will respond? Discuss your ideas with your group.

A child experiments with different colored paints.

VOCABULARY

C 🎧 **2.13** Read and listen to the sentences with words from the conversation. Guess the meaning of each bold word or phrase. Then write the word or phrase next to its definition.

a. Before you submit your answer, you should be **absolutely** sure it is correct.

b. Yuri didn't go to college, but he has years of **hands-on** experience working as a computer programmer.

c. What was Adam's **reaction** when he found out he was accepted to Harvard? Was he excited?

d. Marci is a serious student. If she's not in class, you can **assume** she's sick.

e. The researcher conducted an experiment with over a hundred volunteer **participants.**

f. Our teacher always **encourages** us to do our best. For example, she writes positive comments on our papers.

g. In the research study, people were asked to taste five kinds of yogurt and **rate** them from 1 to 5 (1 = great, 5 = terrible).

h. The limbic system is the part of the brain that **regulates** our emotions, such as anger, fear, and pleasure.

i. Manuel is always busy because he is **involved in** many social, volunteer, and athletic activities.

j. I read a **fascinating** article about the Trans-Siberian Railway, which travels almost 10,000 kilometers from Moscow to Vladivostok. I stayed up late last night reading it.

1. ___fascinating___ (adj) extremely interesting

2. _____ (v) judge or evaluate

3. _____ (v) gives someone hope or support

4. _____ (n) people who take part in a study or activity

5. _____ (n) response; the way people act or feel as a result of something they hear or experience

6. _____ (adv) definitely

7. _____ (adj) connected with or part of (something)

8. _____ (v) guess without proof or evidence

9. _____ (v) controls

10. _____ (adj) practical; related to actual practice rather than theory

D **COMMUNICATE** Work with a partner. Take turns asking and answering these questions.

> A: *Are you **involved in** any clubs, organizations, or activities?*
>
> B: *Yes. I take guitar lessons and play in a band.*

1. Are you **involved in** any clubs, organizations, or activities?

2. Do your friends and family **encourage** you to do your best? How?

3. Have you had any good news lately? What was your family's or friends' **reaction** when you told them?

4. Describe a **fascinating** book you have read or a **fascinating** television program you have watched recently.

5. What was the last movie you saw? How would you **rate** it (excellent, good, OK, etc.)? Explain why you would **rate** it this way.

LISTEN

E 🎧 **2.14** **LISTEN FOR MAIN IDEAS** Read the list of topics. Then listen to the conversation. Check [√] the two topics that the speakers discuss.

1. _____ how curiosity helps babies learn

2. _____ ways that curious people can find answers to their questions

3. _____ characteristics of good parents

4. _____ how to do a science experiment with young children

5. _____ a research study about curiosity and the brain

learn**more** In classrooms in the United States, students are expected to participate in class and express their opinions. One way students participate is by asking questions about what they're learning. Students' questions demonstrate how much they know about the content, as well as their individual perspectives.

F 🎧 **2.15 LISTEN FOR DETAILS** Listen to segment 1 of the conversation. Follow the directions below.

1. Match the descriptions to the speakers. Write N for *Nancy*, D for *David*, and J for *Juan*. (Some descriptions are true for more than one speaker.)

   a. _____ uses Google and Wikipedia every day

   b. _____ enjoys hands-on learning

   c. _____ wanted to know what is inside a golf ball

   d. _____ was told not to ask so many questions in class

   e. _____ thinks that kids learn better when they're curious

2. What question did the researchers at the University of California at Davis want to study? Check [✓] the best choice.

   a. _____ How can teachers help students remember new information?

   b. _____ What happens inside our brains when we are curious?

   c. _____ What kind of information is easiest to remember?

G 🎧 **2.16 LISTEN FOR DETAILS** Listen to segment 2 of the conversation. Follow the directions below.

1. Number the steps in the UC Davis study in the correct order (1–3).

   a. _____ Participants read 100 trivia questions and rated them from 1 to 6.

   b. _____ Researchers tested the participants on the same trivia questions.

   c. _____ Participants read the trivia questions and the answers. At the same time, researchers took pictures of the participants' brains.

2. What did the UC Davis researchers prove? Check [✓] the two correct answers.

   a. _____ The brain responds the same way when we are curious and when someone gives us money or candy.

   b. _____ The hippocampus is the part of the brain that's involved in creating memories.

   c. _____ People remember information better when they are curious.

LISTENING SKILL Make Inferences

When we listen to a speaker, we often understand more than the speaker's exact words. We can make conclusions based on what the speaker says and how he or she says it. This is called *inferring* or *making an inference*. Inferring helps us understand information that a speaker does not say directly.

🎧 **2.17**

Read and listen to the example from the conversation. Can you infer how Nancy felt?

> *But then in fourth grade, I asked so many questions that the teacher, in front of the whole class, told me I could only ask one question every hour.*

We can guess that Nancy felt embarrassed by what the teacher did because she explains that it happened "in front of the whole class."

H 🎧 **2.18** **MAKING INFERENCES** Listen again to segments from the conversation. Write T for statements that are probably *true*. Write F for statements that are probably *false*.

Segment 1

1. _____ David likes to discover things on his own.

2. _____ David wasn't hurt.

3. _____ David's parents didn't worry about his safety.

Segment 2

4. _____ Nancy's preschool teacher encouraged students' curiosity.

5. _____ Nancy's fourth grade teacher was too strict.

6. _____ David approves of Nancy's fourth grade teacher.

Segment 3

7. _____ Curiosity causes the brain to become excited.

8. _____ We probably remember things better when our hippocampus is active.

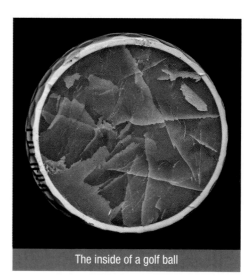
The inside of a golf ball

AFTER YOU LISTEN

I **THINK CRITICALLY Reflect.** Work in a small group. Discuss these questions. Use the information from the conversation and your own ideas to support your answers.

1. Have you ever cut something open or taken it apart in order to see what was inside? If so, what did you discover?

2. How can teachers use students' curiosity to help them learn better?

3. There is a well-known saying in English: "Curiosity killed the cat." Is it possible for curiosity to be harmful? Explain your answer.

SPEAKING

SPEAKING SKILL Show Interest

It is polite to show interest when you are having a conversation with someone. You can do this in two ways:

Use body language. For example, you can nod your head up and down, make eye contact, or smile to show you are interested in the speaker's ideas.

Use expressions and questions. Ask questions or use specific words and expressions like the ones below:

I see.	*Um-hmm.*	*And? (Then what?)*
Really?	*No kidding!*	*That's funny/amazing/incredible/*
Oh, no!	*Wow!*	*awful.*

(See page 168 in the *Independent Student Handbook* for more information on showing interest.)

J 🎧 **2.19** Listen to segments from the conversation. Write the words and expressions that the speakers use to show interest.

1. **Juan:** _____

2. **David:** _____

3. **Nancy:** _____

4. **David:** _____

5. **Nancy:** _____

K **COMMUNICATE** Work with a partner. First, compare your answers to exercise J. Then discuss what body language the speakers could use to express their interest.

L COMMUNICATE Work in a group of three. Tell your classmates three things that they probably don't know about you. Then listen to your classmates and use body language, words, and expressions to show interest.

> A: *OK. First, I was born in Bolivia.*
>
> B: *Really? I didn't know that. I thought you were from Spain.*

PRONUNCIATION SKILL Intonation in Questions

Intonation is the way the voice rises and falls when we speak. *Yes/no* questions and *wh-* questions have different intonation patterns.

🎧 **2.20**

In *yes/no* questions, the intonation usually rises at the end:

Would you say you're a curious person?

In *wh-* questions, the intonation usually falls at the end:

How did they study that?

M 🎧 2.21 Listen to questions from the conversation. Choose *rises* or *falls* according to the intonation you hear at the end of each question. Then listen again and repeat the questions.

1. rises	falls		**4.** rises	falls	
2. rises	falls		**5.** rises	falls	
3. rises	falls		**6.** rises	falls	

N COMMUNICATE Work with a partner. Ask each other the questions below. Add one question you want to ask. Use correct intonation in your questions. Show interest with appropriate words or body language.

> A: *In general, are you a curious person?*
>
> B: *I'm curious about some things, like art. But I'm not very curious about science.*
>
> A: *I see.*

1. In general, are you a curious person? Give an example.
2. What are some ways that you use the Internet to get information?
3. When you were small, did your parents encourage you to ask questions?
4. Have you ever gotten into trouble because you were curious?
5. Your own question _____

O THINK CRITICALLY Interpret an Infographic. People all over the world use Wikipedia to find answers to questions they are curious about. Study the infographic. Then answer the questions.

Facts about Wikipedia

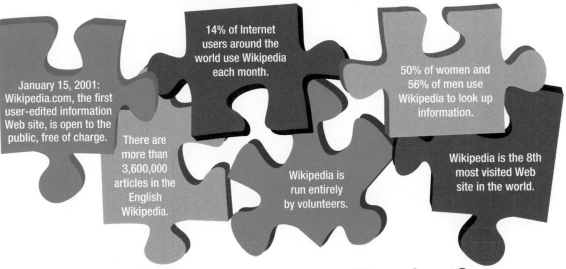

January 15, 2001: Wikipedia.com, the first user-edited information Web site, is open to the public, free of charge.

14% of Internet users around the world use Wikipedia each month.

50% of women and 56% of men use Wikipedia to look up information.

There are more than 3,600,000 articles in the English Wikipedia.

Wikipedia is run entirely by volunteers.

Wikipedia is the 8th most visited Web site in the world.

What subjects are most written about?

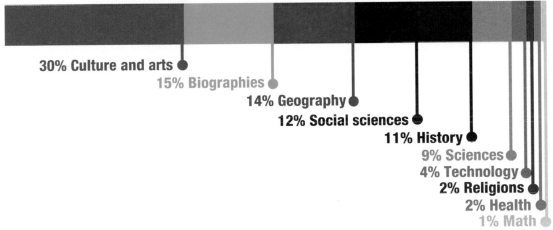

30% Culture and arts
15% Biographies
14% Geography
12% Social sciences
11% History
9% Sciences
4% Technology
2% Religions
2% Health
1% Math

What's the education level of Wikipedia users?

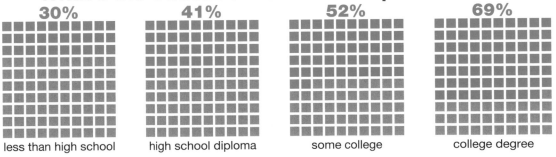

30% less than high school

41% high school diploma

52% some college

69% college degree

1. Who uses Wikipedia more, men or women? Is the difference significant in your opinion?

2. Why do you think people with more education use Wikipedia more?

3. Have you used Wikipedia recently? Was it useful? Explain.

4. What piece of information about Wikipedia is the most surprising to you?

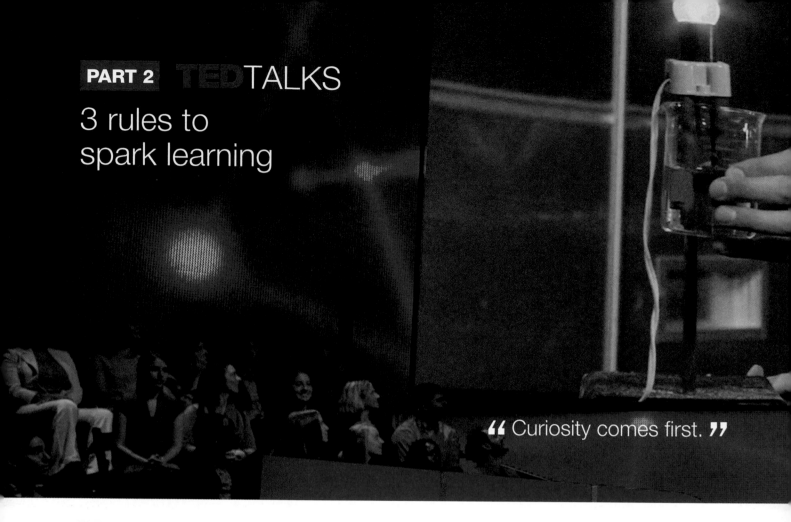

3 rules to spark learning

" Curiosity comes first. "

BEFORE YOU WATCH

A Read the title and information about the TED speaker. A *spark* is a tiny piece of fire. *To spark* means to cause something to happen, like a spark starts a fire. In your experience, what can a good teacher do to spark learning? Tell your class.

> **RAMSEY MUSALLAM** Chemistry Teacher
>
> Ramsey Musallam teaches chemistry at Sacred Heart Cathedral Prep in San Francisco, California. He puts students' inquiry and interests at the center of his teaching, and encourages other teachers to do the same. Musallam is enthusiastic about using technology in education, and he runs an education blog called *Cycles of Learning*. The blog gives written and video tutorials on how to use common apps as effective teaching tools.
>
> Ramsey Musallam's idea worth spreading is that curiosity provides powerful motivation for learning new things, both inside and outside the classroom.

B COMMUNICATE Work with a partner. Discuss these questions.

1. Do you learn best inside or outside of school? Explain your answer.

2. In your primary and secondary schools, was it common for students to raise their hands and ask questions in class? Why, or why not?

3. Which kind of questions are more useful for you?

   a. questions my teacher asks me

   b. questions I ask my teacher

VOCABULARY

C 🎧 **2.22** The sentences below will help you learn words in the TED Talk. Read and listen to the sentences. Then choose the meaning of each bold word or phrase.

1. The students were watching a **demonstration** in chemistry class when the experiment caught fire.

   a. movie

   b. hands-on presentation

   c. slide presentation

2. The professor **extended** the art history lecture by adding examples of paintings from more countries.

   a. made longer

   b. made more interesting

   c. made difficult

3. Because a lunar eclipse is a rare **phenomenon**, we spent several days discussing it in science class.
   a. experiment
   b. danger
   c. event

4. Aki practiced her speech out loud several times, so she was able to get up and speak with **confidence** before an audience of 200 people.
   a. fear
   b. a feeling of security
   c. jokes

5. We were talking about politics when suddenly Marla made a **random** comment about her biology exam.
   a. definite
   b. unrelated
   c. incorrect

6. My grandmother is going to have a surgical **procedure** to help her see more clearly.
   a. exercise
   b. operation
   c. program

7. I used a process of **trial and error** until I finally discovered the solution to the problem.
   a. following directions in a book
   b. learning from another person
   c. trying different things until one works

8. After some **reflection**, she decided to sign up for the advanced chemistry class.
   a. activity
   b. daydreaming
   c. careful thought

9. When I got a C on my research paper, I asked my professor if I could **revise** it and try to get a better grade.
   a. throw something away
   b. change one's mind
   c. fix and improve

10. All people **deserve** the opportunity for an education, even if they don't have a lot of money.
    a. have the right to
    b. expect
    c. plan for

D Read the statements. Check [✓] *Yes* if a statement is true for you and *No* if the statement is not true.

	YES	NO
1. I have learned how to do something by watching a **demonstration.**		
2. I have seen a rare natural **phenomenon.**		
3. I have used **trial and error** to figure out how to do, make, or build something.		
4. When I'm working or studying, I often have **random** thoughts about unrelated topics.		
5. I usually make important decisions after a period of **reflection.**		
6. If I get a low grade on a paper, I ask my teacher if I can **revise** it.		
7. I believe people **deserve** to get the same salary if they have the same job.		

E **COMMUNICATE** Work with a partner. Share your answers from exercise D. Explain or give examples to support your answers. Use the words in bold in your explanations and examples.

The aurora borealis, or "Northern Lights," a natural phenomenon

WATCH

F ▶ **1.29** **WATCH FOR MAIN IDEAS** Watch the edited TED Talk. Check [✓] the statement that summarizes Musallam's main idea.

1. _____ Because chemistry is everywhere, it is important for students to learn it.

2. _____ Technology provides important tools to help teachers do their jobs more effectively.

3. _____ In education, student questions are more valuable than technology or a written curriculum.

4. _____ In some ways, the work of a teacher is harder than the work of a surgeon.

G **THINK CRITICALLY Reflect.** Work with a partner. Compare your answer to exercise F. Then read all the statements. Which ones do you agree with? Explain your answers.

H ▶ **1.30** **WATCH FOR DETAILS** Watch segment 1 of the TED Talk. Choose the best answer to each question.

1. What question was Maddie, Ramsey Musallam's student, probably trying to answer in her experiment at home?
   a. Which scientific theory does this experiment prove?
   b. What will happen if I do the experiment with a candle in the glass?
   c. Will the experiment have a different result if I change the size of the glass?

2. How did Musallam feel about Maddie's experiment?
   a. He loved it.
   b. He thought it was ridiculous.
   d. He disapproved of it.

3. What fascinated Musallam?
   a. The effect of temperature on the results of the experiment
   b. The candle inside the beaker
   c. The fact that Maddie asked a new question

WORDS IN THE TALK
aneurysm (n): a dangerous weakness in the wall of an artery, such as the aorta
aorta (n): the large blood vessel that brings blood from the heart to the rest of the body
buzzword (n): a word or phrase from a specific industry that becomes very popular for a period of time

NOTE-TAKING SKILL Use a T-Chart

A T-chart is a kind of graphic organizer. It is useful for comparing two concepts, things, situations, or events. For example, this T-chart compares the advantages and disadvantages of hands-on learning.

Hands-on learning	
Advantages	**Disadvantages**
1. Uses all the senses (sight, touch, etc.)	1. Requires many types of materials
2. Encourages student participation	2. May be more difficult to manage large classes
3. Helps memory	3. Requires more teacher time to prepare

I ▶ **1.31** **WATCH AND TAKE NOTES** Watch segment 2. Then use the T-chart to complete the surgeon's rules for performing surgery and Musallam's rules for being a good teacher.

SURGEON'S RULES	MUSALLAM'S RULES
1. Ask _____ questions about the procedure.	1. _____ comes first. _____ can be windows to great instruction.
2. _____ the messy process of trial and error.	2. _____ the mess.
3. Practice intense _____ to design and _____ the procedure.	3. Practice _____.

J **COMMUNICATE** Work with a partner. Compare your answers from exercise H. Explain the surgeon's and Musallam's rules in your own words. Then compare the two lists. How are they similar or different?

K THINK CRITICALLY Infer. Work with a partner. Read the quotes below from the edited TED Talk. Discuss these questions: What is the usual meaning of each bold word? What is its meaning in the talk?

1. "Questions and curiosity like Maddie's are **magnets** that draw us towards our teachers."

   A magnet is a piece of metal that attracts other metals so that they stick to it. In the talk, Musallam means that questions and curiosity make students interested in what the teachers are saying.

2. "Student questions are the **seeds** of real learning."

3. "Learning is **ugly**."

4. "Questions can be **windows** to great instruction."

5. "Can we be the **surgeons** of our classrooms?"

L ▶ 1.32 EXPAND YOUR VOCABULARY Watch the excerpts from the TED Talk. Guess the meanings of the words and phrases in the box.

> spacing out   geek out   snap me out of   was freaked out

M WATCH MORE Go to TED.com to watch the TED Talk by Ramsey Musallam.

AFTER YOU WATCH

N REFLECT Work with a partner. Discuss these questions.

1. Do you think "learning is ugly"? If so, what kinds of learning are ugly? Explain your answer.

2. What are some similarities between a surgeon and a teacher? What are some differences?

3. Would you like to have Ramsey Musallam as your teacher? Why, or why not?

4. Think about your own teachers. Have you ever had a teacher who encouraged you to be curious? Explain.

Put It Together

A **THINK CRITICALLY** **Synthesize.** Work with a partner. Answer the following questions.

1. In Part 1, David told the story of cutting open a golf ball. Would Musallam be happy if he were David's father? Why, or why not?

2. In Part 1, Nancy said that her teacher limited her to one question every hour. What would Musallam say to this teacher?

B **THINK CRITICALLY** **Personalize.** Discuss the questions in your groups.

1. Have you ever been curious about the same questions as David, Maddie, and Nancy? Explain.

2. What is one thing you are curious about? How could you find the answer (without using the Internet or a book)?

A brother and sister generate light from wind power in Zeeland, Netherlands.

COMMUNICATE

ASSIGNMENT: Give an Individual Presentation You will give an individual presentation about a time when your curiosity led you to learn or try something new. Review the ideas in Parts 1 and 2 and the listening and speaking skills as you prepare your presentation.

PREPARE

C Plan your presentation. Think about a time when your curiosity led you to learn or try something new. Make notes in the chart. Then share your notes with a partner.

1. What were you curious about, or what question did you want to answer?	
2. How did you find the answer? What was it?	
3. How did you feel about your discovery?	

PRESENTATION SKILL Consider Your Audience

An audience is the group of people who listen to a talk or presentation. It is useful to think about the characteristics of your specific audience when you are planning a presentation. Use questions like these to help you:

- Where are my listeners from? How old are they? What is their cultural and educational background?
- What do they already know about my topic?
- What special information or vocabulary do I need to explain?
- How can I make my topic interesting to this particular group of listeners?

(See page 174 in the *Independent Student Handbook* for more information on considering your audience.)

D ▶ **1.33** Watch the segment from the talk. Musallam says, "We're all teachers. We know learning is ugly." Why does Musallam use the word *we*? What does he assume about his audience? What did he do to make his talk interesting for this group of listeners? Discuss your ideas with a partner.

E COLLABORATE Work with a partner. Practice your presentation. Use your notes from the chart in exercise C.

F Read the rubric on page 182 before you present. Notice how your presentation will be evaluated. Keep these categories in mind as you present and watch your classmates' presentations.

PRESENT

G Give your presentation to a small group. Watch your classmates' presentations. After you watch each one, provide feedback using the rubric as a guide. Add notes and any other feedback you want to share.

H THINK CRITICALLY Evaluate. In your group, discuss the feedback you received. As a class, discuss what you did well and what might make your presentation even stronger.

REFLECT

Reflect on what you have learned. Check [✓] your progress.

I can
- ☐ make inferences when listening.
- ☐ show interest during a conversation.
- ☐ use correct question intonation.
- ☐ use a T-chart for taking notes.
- ☐ consider my audience when I plan a presentation.

I understand the meanings of these words and phrases and can use them.
Circle those you know. Underline those you need to work on.

absolutely	deserve	hands-on	procedure AWL	reflection
assume AWL	encourage	involved in AWL	random AWL	regulate AWL
confidence	extend	participant AWL	rate	revise AWL
demonstration AWL	fascinating	phenomenon AWL	reaction AWL	trial and error

The Livable City

A vertical garden on the Quai Branly Museum in Paris, France

THINK AND DISCUSS

1 Read the unit title. What is a "livable city"?

2 Look at the photo and read the caption. What is the connection between the unit title and this building?

BEFORE YOU LISTEN

A COMMUNICATE Work in a small group. Discuss these questions.

1. Look at the photo. What kind of place is this? Where do you think it is? What do you think people do in this place?

2. Describe a big city near you.

3. Do you live in a big city? If yes, do you like living there? Why, or why not? If not, do you want to live in a big city? Why, or why not?

B 🎧 **2.23 COLLABORATE** You will listen to a lecture about public space and the livable city. Listen to an excerpt from the beginning of the lecture. Then with your group, answer the professor's question: *What's a "livable" city?*

Bedzed in London is the UK's first large-scale environmentally friendly community with homes, offices, a college, and community facilities.

VOCABULARY

C 🎧 **2.24** Read and listen to the sentences with words from the lecture. Guess the meaning of each bold word or phrase. Then write each word or phrase next to its definition.

a. San Francisco is an **attractive** city. It has beautiful views and good-looking buildings.

b. Cities that have large **public** parks include Mexico City and Moscow. People who live in these cities can use the parks for free.

c. A museum exhibit can **draw** a big crowd of people. For example, over 154,000 people came to the "Titanic" exhibit at the National Mississippi River Museum.

d. Cities that have safe places to walk and exercise help people to **lead** healthier lives.

e. The Walt Disney Concert Hall is a famous **performance center** in Los Angeles, California. You can see orchestras from all over the world there.

f. Many cities provide places for teens to **hang out.** At these places, they can meet friends and participate in activities, such as rock climbing and other sports.

g. An open **sewer** is a danger to public health. In modern cities, underground pipes safely carry waste water away from homes and businesses.

h. Paris-Plage is an area for **recreation** on the River Seine in Paris, France. It has a sandy beach, a swimming pool, and areas for inline skating, playing volleyball, and other activities.

i. San Francisco **residents** enjoy city life. Most of the people who live there like living in a big city.

j. Cars and **pedestrians** both need to watch out for each other in order to make city streets safe. Walkers and drivers are both responsible for avoiding accidents.

1. _____pedestrians_____ (n) people walking on a sidewalk, across a street, or down a road

2. _____ (v) attract

3. _____ (adj) nice-looking

4. _____ (v) spend time in a place

5. _____ (n) fun things to do, such as sports, hobbies, and amusements

6. _____ (n) a place for presentations of ceremonies or works of art (drama, music, dance, etc.) for an audience

7. _____ (n) people who live in a certain place

8. _____ (adj) meant for use by the people

9. _____ (v) experience

10. _____ (n) a tunnel or pipe that carries waste and liquid from kitchens and showers

D COMMUNICATE Work with a partner. Take turns asking and answering the questions. Use the words in **bold** in your answers.

> A: *What types of **recreation** do you enjoy most?*
>
> B: *For **recreation**, I like to go swimming and play volleyball.*

1. What types of **recreation** do you enjoy most?

2. In your opinion, what is the most **attractive** city in the world? Why?

3. Where do you and your friends usually **hang out** on the weekends?

4. Have you ever been to a **performance center?** Where? What did you see there?

5. Are there any streets just for **pedestrians** in your city? Are pedestrian-only streets a good idea? Why, or why not?

LISTEN

E 🎧 **2.25** ▶ **1.34** **LISTEN FOR MAIN IDEAS** Read the statements. Then listen to the lecture. Check [✓] the statement that best expresses the main idea of the entire lecture.

1. _____ Public spaces should be clean and attractive.

2. _____ Factoría Joven is an example of a good public space.

3. _____ Public spaces can make cities more livable.

4. _____ Good public spaces improve the environment.

5. _____ Good public spaces draw people together.

Skateboarding at Factoría Joven

LISTENING SKILL Listen for Problems and Solutions

Recognizing problems and connecting them with their solutions is an important listening skill. To recognize and connect problems and solutions, listen for the following signal words and phrases:

Signals for Problems:

The / One problem / issue / challenge (with . . .) is . . .

Signals for Solutions:

The / One solution / answer / response is . . .

This . . . solves / addresses / deals with the problem

F 🎧 **2.26** **LISTEN FOR DETAILS** Listen to three excerpts from the lecture. Match each place with the problem it solves. There is one extra problem.

PLACE	PROBLEM
1. _____ Factoria Joven	**a.** bad air
2. _____ Cheonggyecheon Park	**b.** lack of fresh food
3. _____ Gosford Glow Footpath	**c.** lack of activities for young people
	d. dangerous areas

G 🎧 **2.27** **LISTEN FOR DETAILS** Listen to segments from the lecture. Match each detail in the box with the correct public space. Write the letters of the details in the correct places in the mind map below.

a. was designed for young people	d. has walls you can paint on	g. saves electricity
b. is open 24 hours a day	e. was covered by a freeway	h. makes walking safer
c. is in Australia	f. is in Spain	i. is in South Korea

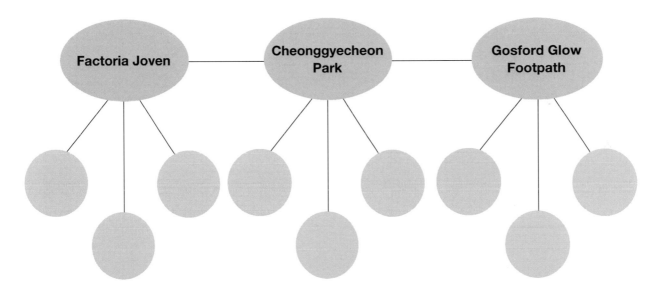

H **COMMUNICATE** Work in a small group. Discuss your answers to these questions. Give reasons for your answers.

1. Which public space described in the lecture would you like to visit? Why?

2. Which one do you think is the most interesting? Why?

3. Which one is the most useful? Why?

AFTER YOU LISTEN

I **THINK CRITICALLY Reflect.** Work in a small group. Look at the list of characteristics (typical qualities) that make a public space more livable. Then complete the Venn diagram by answering the questions.

a. is safe

b. has activities for people to do

c. attracts people

d. helps make the environment healthier

e. helps people connect with nature

f. saves energy

g. adds beauty

1. What characteristics do Factoria Joven, Cheonggyecheon Park, and Gosford Glow Path have in common? Write the letters in the space where the three circles overlap.

2. Which characteristics do two of the places share? Write those letters in the spaces where the two circles overlap.

3. Finally, do any characteristics belong to just one place? Write those letters in the space where the circles do not overlap.

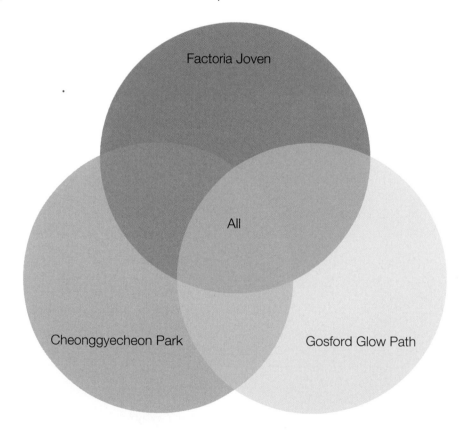

4. Now discuss your answer to this question with your group:

   Which characteristic do you think is the most important one for a public space to have?

Cheonggyecheon Stream, Seoul, South Korea

SPEAKING

SPEAKING SKILL Talk about Solutions

To talk about solutions, speakers use the words and phrases you learned in the Listening Skill box on page 126. When using these signal words and phrases, you should try to vary your word choice to avoid too much repetition.

For example:

> **One issue** in big cities is the lack of space. High-rise buildings can **address** this **problem**. Tall buildings **solve** this **issue** by taking up vertical space, which is unlimited. Another **response** is creating public spaces. Public spaces are a good **solution** because they provide people with places to meet outside their homes.

J **THINK CRITICALLY** **Analyze.** Work in a small group. Think about the conditions in big cities. Look at the list of issues below and add two of your own ideas. Then think of two possible solutions for each issue.

ISSUES	POSSIBLE SOLUTIONS	
crime	1. _____	2. _____
crowds	1. _____	2. _____
traffic	1. _____	2. _____
noise	1. _____	2. _____
your idea	1. _____	2. _____
your idea	1. _____	2. _____

K Report to the class your possible solutions to the issues in exercise J. Use solution words and phrases.

A: *One issue in big cities is crime. A good solution is better street lights.*

B: *Another response to crime is to have more police officers.*

PRONUNCIATION SKILL Linking

English speakers often connect words when they talk. For example, they often connect the final consonant sound of one word to the first vowel sound in the next word. This makes the two words sound like one word. This is called **linking**.

It's important to recognize linking sounds so you can better understand English speakers. Also, if you link sounds, your speech will sound more natural.

Listen to how the following words are linked.

🎧 **2.28** first of all   what's a   some are

L 🎧 **2.29** Listen to some sentences from the lecture. Draw lines to connect the linked sounds.

1. These are common problems.

2. It's attractive.

3. It attracts about 150 young people each day.

4. Let's take a look at some examples.

5. They also solve other problems of city life.

M 🎧 **2.30** Listen and complete the sentences with the words you hear.

1. _____ Merida, Spain.

2. _____ the outside.

3. And that's what we're going to _____ today.

4. Then it became _____ sewer.

5. People come to the _____ night, just to look at it.

N Work with a partner. Take turns reading the sentences in exercises L and M with linked sounds.

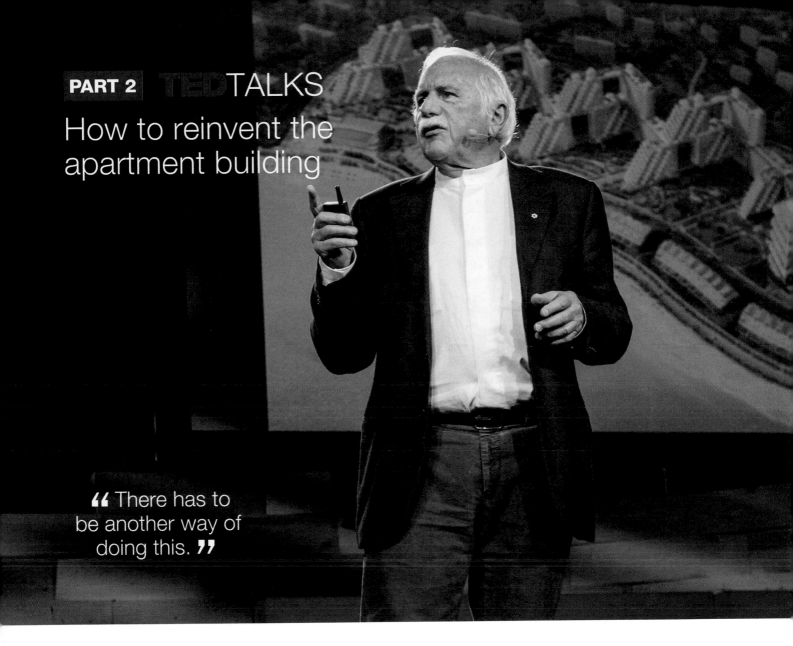

How to reinvent the apartment building

❝ There has to be another way of doing this. ❞

BEFORE YOU WATCH

A THINK CRITICALLY Predict. Read the title and information about the TED speaker. *Reinvent* means to do something in a new way. Why might the TED speaker want to reinvent apartment buildings? Tell your class.

MOSHE SAFDIE Architect

Moshe Safdie is an Israeli/Canadian/American architect. He designs apartments, museums, airports, and other structures. He is interested in public spaces that improve cities and towns. Safdie also builds apartments that let in natural light and include lots of open space and gardens. He wants his apartments to help people connect to nature, even when they live in big, crowded cities.

Moshe Safdie's idea worth spreading is that we can plan today for livable cities of the future. We can create apartment buildings and other structures that connect people more closely with each other and with the natural world.

B COMMUNICATE Work with a partner. Discuss your answers to the questions.

> A: *Apartment buildings in big cities often have a main front door. They usually don't have gardens.*
>
> B: *Actually, they often don't have much space around them at all.*

1. Describe the typical apartment building in a large city. What does it look like?

2. What are some good things about living in a big apartment building in a large city? What are some bad things?

3. In his TED Talk, Safdie talks about both urban (city) areas and suburbs, small cities or towns outside large cities. What are some good things about living in a suburb? What are some bad things?

VOCABULARY

C 🎧 **2.31** The sentences below will help you learn words and phrases in the TED Talk. Read and listen to the sentences. Choose the meaning of each bold word or phrase.

1. Safdie designs **middle-income** housing projects. They might be too expensive for some people, but you don't have to be rich to live in them.
   a. high-income **b.** average-income **c.** low-income

2. It costs a lot to live in Tokyo and San Francisco. However, Mumbai, India, is one of the most **affordable** cities in the world.
   a. crowded **b.** dangerous **c.** inexpensive

3. People who live in the suburbs have to drive a lot. One way to **sustain** the suburbs is to move businesses into them so people don't have to drive so much.
   a. visit **b.** keep **c.** destroy

4. The Outdoor Sculpture Collection at Western Washington University is a public space that is **integrated with** an outdoor art gallery. Students can sit and talk and enjoy art at the same time.
   a. separated from **b.** combined with **c.** inside of

5. We need to look at city living in a new way. For example, we need to **rethink** the way we create housing in crowded cities.
   a. reconsider **b.** forget **c.** remind

6. Safdie built a unique housing project: Each **unit** is like a house. Residents don't feel like their home is attached to another person's home.
   a. apartment **b.** amount **c.** project

7. The population **density** of large cities gave Safdie an idea: Can we build housing projects that don't feel crowded, even if the city itself is crowded?
   a. cost **b.** amount of crime **c.** closeness

8. It costs a lot of money to live in Tokyo. For example, it's **extremely** expensive to buy an apartment there.

    a. somewhat   **b.** very   **c.** not at all

9. The architects took an old office building and completely **reconfigured** it. They put shops on the ground floor and apartments on the top floors.

    a. changed the structure   **b.** destroyed it   **c.** kept the original design

10. A popular **concept** in architecture is creating spaces that help people connect with nature.

    a. issue   **b.** project   **c.** idea

D COMMUNICATE Work in a small group. Read and answer the questions. Use the words in bold in your answers.

> A: *What is your idea of the perfect housing* **unit**? *What features does it have?*
>
> B: *The perfect housing* **unit** *is big and has lots of windows.*

1. What is your idea of the perfect housing **unit**? What features does it have?

2. Where do **middle-income** families live in your area?

3. What are some examples of **affordable** places to live? What makes them affordable?

4. What are some popular **concepts** about making cities more livable?

WATCH

E ▶ **1.35 WATCH FOR MAIN IDEAS** Watch segment 1 of the edited TED Talk. What is the issue that Safdie describes? What is the solution? Check [✓] the correct answers.

Issue

1. _____ The need to make cities less crowded and more like suburbs

2. _____ The need to improve life for people who live in apartments

3. _____ The need to let more light into apartments

Solution

1. _____ Move people out of cities.

2. _____ Add gardens to apartments.

3. _____ Make apartments like houses.

WORDS IN THE TALK
prevailing (adj): having the most influence
promenades (n): special areas for walking

F THINK CRITICALLY Infer. In segment 1, Safdie refers to public high-rise buildings in cities such as New York and Philadelphia, and to the people "who have no choice" about living in them. Work with a partner. Discuss your answers to these questions.

1 Who do you think Safdie is describing?

2 Why do some people have no choice about where they live?

The Marina Bay Sands hotel complex in Marina Bay, Singapore, designed by Moshe Safdie

learn**more** Most new homes that were built in the U.S. during the 1960s were in suburbs, large areas outside of big cities. It was part of the "American Dream" to leave the city and live in the suburbs, where the air was clean and the schools were good. In the suburbs, homes were far from businesses. Also, there often was no public transportation, so people had to drive everywhere. This is still true today in many U.S. suburbs, but good public transportation and walkable areas are now being developed.

G ▶ **1.36** **WATCH FOR DETAILS** Watch segment 2 of the edited TED Talk. As you watch, pay attention to details that explain how Habitat solves the problem Safdie is concerned about. Complete the notes with words from the box. You can use some words more than once.

urban	apartments	garden	public	community
incomes	three hours	parks	longest	light

New York City, U.S.

_____ above offices
1

gardens and open space for the _____
2

each apartment has its own _____
3

lets in lots of _____
4

Qinhuangdao, China

for people with middle _____
5

each apartment lets in _____ of light in winter
6

Singapore (1st example) & Colombo, Sri Lanka

also for people with average _____
7

has gardens, _____ streets, and _____
8   9

Singapore (2nd example)

promenades and parks integrated with _____ life
10

_____ gardens
11

"sky park" with jogging paths, restaurants, and the world's _____
12
swimming pool

NOTE-TAKING SKILL Review Your Notes

When you take notes during a presentation, you should review them soon afterward to make sure you understand them. If you remember more information, add it to your notes. If you didn't understand something or you think you might have missed some important information, ask a classmate or your teacher for help. Look at the example of notes the student took in Exercise G.

Singapore (1st example) & Colombo, Sri Lanka

also for people with average _incomes_

gardens, **????** streets, and _parks_

Now notice how two students discuss their notes.

A: *For the first Singapore example, I didn't get the type of streets. What do you have?*

B: *I have "community" . . . "community streets."*

A: *Oh, okay. Thanks.*

H **CHECK YOUR NOTES** Review your notes. Did you get everything? Compare your notes with a partner. Ask your partner questions about any answers that you are not sure about.

I ▶ **1.37** **EXPAND YOUR VOCABULARY** Watch the excerpts from the TED Talk. Guess the meanings of the phrases in the box.

> are prevailing   came up with   and so on and so forth   touch on

J **WATCH MORE** Go to TED.com to watch the full TED talk by Moshe Safdie.

AFTER YOU WATCH

K **THINK CRITICALLY** Infer. In his talk, Safdie says, "We can't sustain suburbs, so let's design a building which gives the qualities of a house to each unit." Work with a partner. Discuss your answers to these questions.

1. Why do you think Safdie says that we can't sustain suburbs?

2. What are some "qualities of a house" that Safdie mentions?

L THINK CRITICALLY Interpret an Infographic. Work with a partner. Look at the infographic and chart. Discuss your answers to these questions.

1. Between which years does the infographic show changes in livability?
2. Which five cities became less livable during this period?
3. Which three cities became more livable during this period?
4. Which country had the greatest number of livable cities in 2015?
5. What characteristics is the livability index based on?

The World's Most Livable Cities

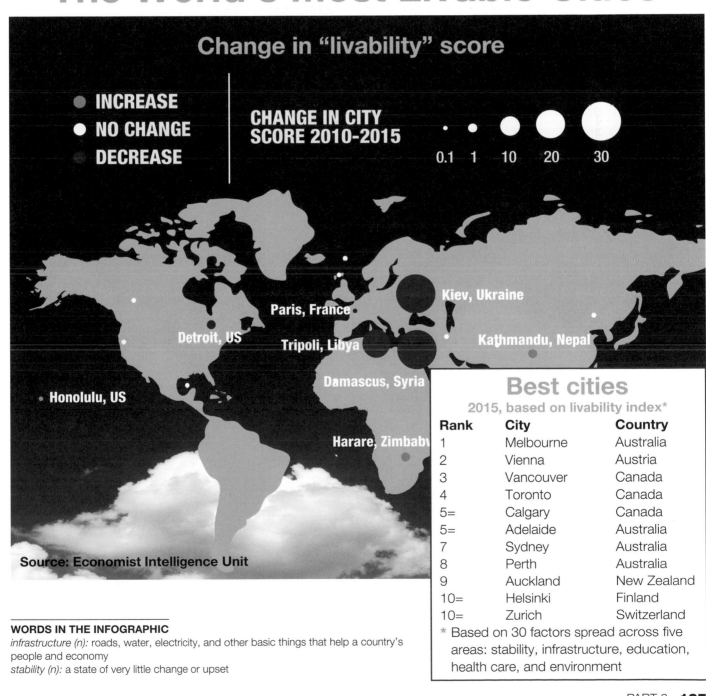

Change in "livability" score

- INCREASE
- NO CHANGE
- DECREASE

CHANGE IN CITY SCORE 2010-2015

0.1   1   10   20   30

Kiev, Ukraine

Paris, France

Detroit, US

Kathmandu, Nepal

Tripoli, Libya

Damascus, Syria

Honolulu, US

Harare, Zimbabwe

Source: Economist Intelligence Unit

Best cities
2015, based on livability index*

Rank	City	Country
1	Melbourne	Australia
2	Vienna	Austria
3	Vancouver	Canada
4	Toronto	Canada
5=	Calgary	Canada
5=	Adelaide	Australia
7	Sydney	Australia
8	Perth	Australia
9	Auckland	New Zealand
10=	Helsinki	Finland
10=	Zurich	Switzerland

* Based on 30 factors spread across five areas: stability, infrastructure, education, health care, and environment

WORDS IN THE INFOGRAPHIC

infrastructure (n): roads, water, electricity, and other basic things that help a country's people and economy

stability (n): a state of very little change or upset

Put It Together

A **THINK CRITICALLY** **Synthesize.** Work in a small group. Answer these questions. Use examples from the lecture in Part 1 and the TED Talk in Part 2 in your discussion.

1. What did planners do to make cities more livable?

2. In your opinion, which of the planners' ideas is the most useful or important? Why?

B **THINK CRITICALLY** **Analyze.** Are there any public spaces, buildings, or other projects in your area that are similar to the ones in the Part 1 lecture or the TED Talk? If yes, list them. Explain how they draw people together, increase safety, help people connect with nature, or make your area more livable in some way. If no, propose a space, building, or other project that your community should consider.

COMMUNICATE

ASSIGNMENT: Give an Individual Presentation You will give an individual presentation about a building or public space that makes a city or town more livable. Explain how this building or space solves a problem of city living.

Parisians and tourists at Paris Plage on the bank of the Seine River in Paris, France

PREPARE

PRESENTATION SKILL Organize a Problem–Solution Presentation

There are several ways to organize a presentation about a problem and its solution. Two options are given below. With either, remember to start with some background information so the audience understands the context.

1. **Describe the problem first and then explain the solution.**

   Introduction: Background information-Gosford is a city on the coast of New South Wales in Australia.

   Problem: Needed a safe way for people to cross the railroad tracks

   Solution: Created a beautiful, energy-efficient, lighted path

2. **Describe the solution first and then suggest how it solves a problem.**

   Introduction: Background information-Gosford is a city on the coast of New South Wales in Australia.

   Solution: Built a lighted path that uses minerals

   Problem solved: No safe way for people to cross the railroad tracks

C COLLABORATE Think about your answers in exercise B. Choose your topic. Decide if you are going to talk about a building or a public space.

D Decide how you will organize your problem-solution presentation. Choose option 1 or option 2 below and complete the outline with information about your topic.

OPTION 1

Topic: (What is the name of the building or public space?)

_____

1. Introduction: (Where is it? Or: Where will it be?)

   _____

2. Problem(s): (What problem(s) does your building or public space solve?)

   _____

   _____

3. Solution: (Explain in detail how your building or public space solves or will solve the problem(s).)

   _____

   _____

A biker rides along a path in Amsterdam that glows with solar-powered lights.

OPTION 2

Topic: (What is the name of the building or public space?)

_____

1. Introduction: (Where is it? Or: Where will it be?)

_____

_____

2. Solution: (Describe the solution: What it is/what it will be, what it does/what it will do, and other interesting features about it.)

_____

_____

3. How it solved the problem(s): (Explain in detail how your building or public space solved or will solve the problem(s).)

_____

_____

E PRACTICE Work with a partner. Practice your presentation. As you practice:

- Use problem–solution words to introduce problems and describe solutions.
- Remember to link words.

F Read the rubric on page 183 before you present. Notice how your presentation will be evaluated. Keep these categories in mind as you present and watch your classmates' presentations.

PRESENT

G Give your presentation to a small group. Watch your classmates' presentations. After you watch each one, provide feedback using the rubric as a guide. Add notes or any other feedback you want to share.

H THINK CRITICALLY Evaluate. In a small group, discuss the feedback you received. Discuss what you did well and what might make your presentation stronger.

REFLECT

Reflect on what you have learned. Check [✓] your progress.

I can

☐ listen for problems and solutions.
☐ talk about solutions.
☐ understand and use linking.
☐ review my notes.
☐ organize a problem–solution presentation.

I understand the meanings of these words and phrases and can use them.
Circle those you know. Underline those you need to work more on.

affordable	extremely	pedestrian	resident AWL
attractive	hang out	performance space	rethink
concept AWL	integrate with AWL	public	sewer
density	lead	reconfigure	sustain AWL
draw	middle-income AWL	recreation	unit

UNIT 8

Life Lessons

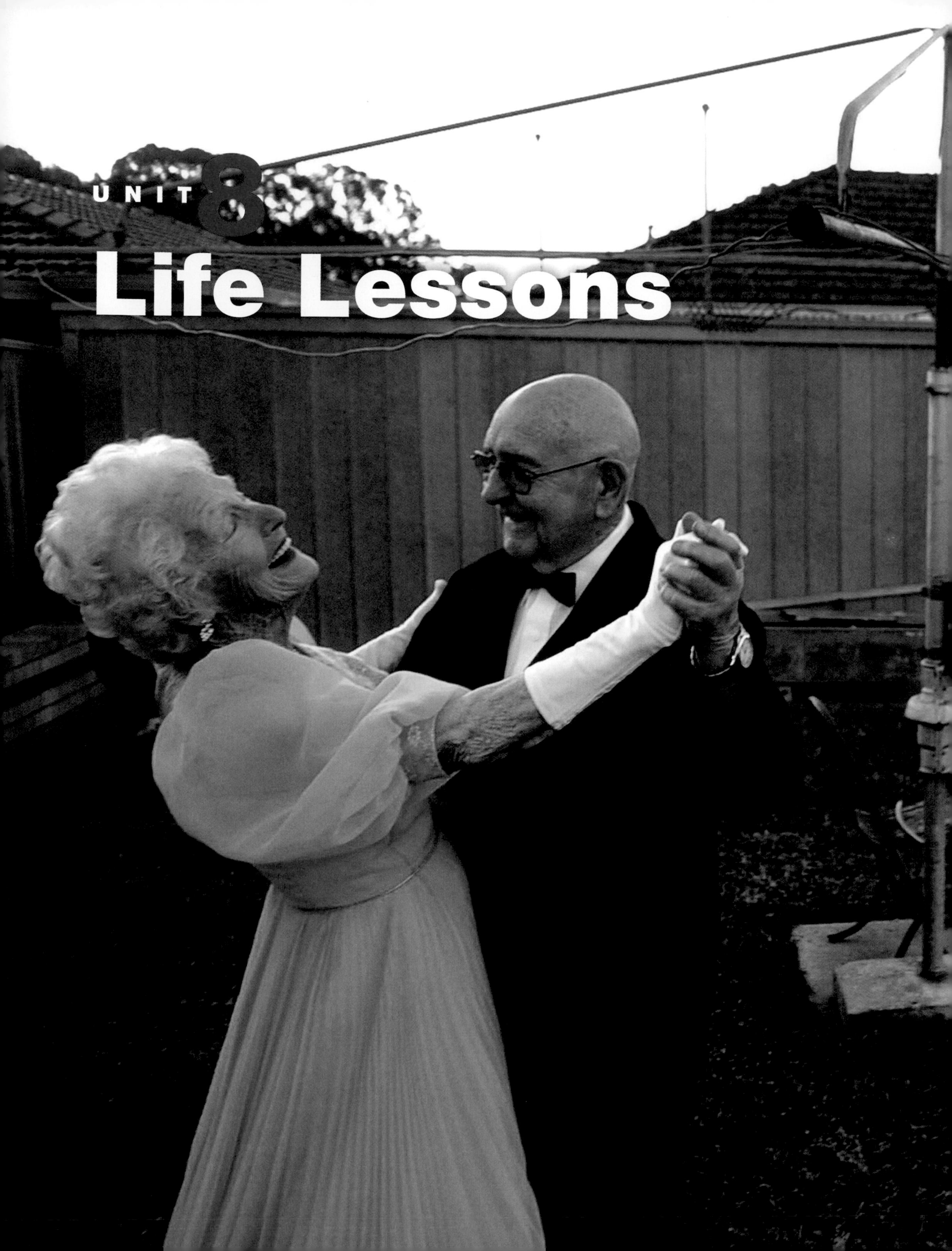

1 Read the unit title. What do you think *life lessons* are?

2 Look at the photo and read the caption. How do you think the two people are feeling? What lessons do you think they have learned in their lives?

Friends for over 40 years, ballroom dancers Mary Hall and Gerald Kavanagh practice on a warm spring day in Bendigo, Australia.

BEFORE YOU LISTEN

A **COMMUNICATE** Work in a small group. Discuss these questions.

1. What would you like to change about your life, for example, your habits or the way that you do things? Why do you want to change these things?

2. Think about a time when you made a change in your life. Was it easy or hard? Explain your answer.

3. Look at the photo. What reasons might these people have to explore Antarctica?

B **2.32** **COLLABORATE** Think about the title of the lecture *How to Change Your Life* and listen to the first part. What answers do the students give to the professor's question, "What kinds of changes do people often want to make in their lives?" Think of some more examples of changes. Discuss your ideas with your group.

Members of an expedition team walk over ice in Queen Maud Land, Antarctica.

VOCABULARY

C Match each word with its definition.

1. __d__ accomplish (v)

2. _____ avoid (v)

3. _____ behavior (n)

4. _____ desire (n)

5. _____ expert (n)

6. _____ factor (n)

7. _____ principle (n)

8. _____ punishment (n)

9. _____ reinforce (v)

10. _____ reward (n)

a. a payment someone must make for doing wrong

b. something to consider

c. to make stronger

d. to achieve

e. a person who is very knowledgeable about a particular subject

f. a strong wish

g. an award or present for doing something good

h. to stay away from

i. rule

j. a way of acting

D 🎧 **2.33** Complete each sentence with the correct form of a word from exercise C. Then listen and check your answers.

1. Cost is an important _____ factor _____ to consider when you are choosing a college.

2. If you have a strong _____ to change your life, you will find a way to do it.

3. The _____ for studying hard is getting good grades.

4. If you want to _____ being late for an appointment, leave earlier.

5. The _____ for stealing is going to jail.

6. A study showed that one _____ that many students want to change is staying up very late at night.

7. _____ say that students who get enough sleep have better grades.

8. Two _____ for having a happy life include treating people kindly and having an "attitude of gratitude."

9. It can be difficult to _____ your goals if you don't make a plan.

10. One way to _____ your understanding of a new word is to try to use it five times a day.

E COMMUNICATE Work with a partner. Take turns asking and answering the questions. Use the words in bold in your answers.

> A: *What do you try to **avoid** and how?*
>
> B: *I try to **avoid** eating too many sweets. I always carry a healthy snack.*

1. What do you try to **avoid**? How do you do this?

2. What are your **principles** for having a happy life?

3. What goal do you hope to **accomplish** this year? In the next five years?

4. What are some of your biggest **desires**? Why?

5. Do you think parents should give children **rewards** for good **behavior?** Why, or why not?

6. What is an important **factor** in choosing your major (or field of study)?

7. What's a good way to **reinforce** the new vocabulary you learn?

LISTEN

F 🎧 **2.34** ▶ **1.38** **LISTEN FOR MAIN IDEAS** Read the list of topics. Then listen to the lecture. Check [√] the two main topics of the lecture.

1. _____ Two Types of Motivation

2. _____ Motivation and Making Changes

3. _____ The Role of Keeping a Journal

4. _____ Staying Positive When Making Changes

5. _____ Principles for Making Changes

NOTE-TAKING SKILL **Record Definitions**

Academic lectures often include definitions of terms that might be new to you. It is important to understand and record the new words. They help you to understand the content, and you often need to know them for tests.

When you hear a new word, write it with its definition next to it (in note form, not in a complete sentence). It's a good idea to ask the lecturer to write new words on the board so you can see how they're spelled.

It's also helpful to add an example or further explanation of the term. The lecturer might give one, or you might need to think of your own.

Example:

strategy: planning in order to achieve a goal

Ex: making flashcards to learn new words

G 🎧 **2.35** **LISTEN FOR DETAILS** Listen to segment 1 of the lecture. Complete these notes on the definitions that you hear.

1. *motivation:* _____the desire to do things_____

2. *extrinsic motivation:* motivation from _____

   Ex: doing things in order to get a _____ or to

   _____ punishment

3. *intrinsic motivation:* motivation from _____

   Ex: doing things for their own sake because they're _____

LISTENING SKILL **Listen for Listing Words and Phrases**

Speakers often use listing words and phrases to list ideas. For example, perhaps they are explaining three ways to change or several different methods for staying motivated. These words and phrases help the listener focus on and understand important ideas.

Here are some common listing words and phrases:

First, First of all, The first thing (I want to mention is . . .)

Second, Secondly,

Then,

Next,

Another (idea/thing) is ...

In addition,

Finally, Lastly,

H 🎧 **2.36** Listen to segment 2 of the lecture. Complete each principle with the listing word you hear.

Principles for Making Changes

1. _____, be positive.

2. _____, pay attention to the process.

3. _____, break the process into smaller parts.

I Complete the chart with the letters of the examples.

Examples

a. keep a journal

b. start enjoying extra free time

c. make a list of all things that will help him

PRINCIPLES FOR MAKING CHANGES		
Principle 1	Principle 2	Principle 3
Example: To get to class on time, Sam can _____.	Example: If Sam starts getting to class on time, he'll _____.	Example: _____

AFTER YOU LISTEN

J   THINK CRITICALLY Personalize. Work in a small group. Review the examples the lecturer gave for intrinsic and extrinsic motivation in exercise G on page 147. Then discuss these questions.

1. What are some things that you do because of intrinsic motivation?

2. What are some things that you do because of extrinsic motivation?

SPEAKING

SPEAKING SKILL Rephrase Key Ideas

Rephrasing means saying something again, but using different words. To be sure your listeners understand what you are saying, it's a good idea to repeat or rephrase your key ideas.

Here are some common expressions you can use to introduce rephrasing:

that is

in other words

that is to say

You can also just follow the word or idea with the rephrasing.

Examples:

<u>Break the new behavior into smaller parts.</u> **That is,** <u>turn it into a series of small steps.</u>
          idea   rephrase

<u>Break the new behavior into smaller parts</u>—<u>a series of small steps instead of one big one.</u>
          idea   rephrase

K   Work with a partner. Read these sentences from the lecture. Underline the information the speaker rephrases. Draw two lines under the rephrasing. Put a check [✓] over any expressions that introduce rephrasing.

1. People who have intrinsic motivation do things for their own sake. That is, they do a thing because the thing itself is a reward.

2. This helps to reinforce a new behavior. In other words, it helps to make a new behavior a habit.

3. You need to enjoy the process of change. Find pleasure in the new behavior.

L COLLABORATE Choose one of the topics below. Then in a small group, take turns talking about your topics. When you are telling the group about your topic, rephrase at least one word or idea. Use the expressions from the Speaking Skill box on page 149.

Before I leave for school each morning, I always check WhatsApp. That is, I check my phone to see if there are any messages from my family.

Topics:

1. Explain what you do to get ready for school or work in the morning.

2. Explain your principles for one of the following:

   - being a better student
   - saving money
   - being a good friend
   - leading a healthy lifestyle
   - meeting people

PRONUNCIATION SKILL Vowels in Unstressed Syllables

Vowels in unstressed syllables usually do not have their full sound. Instead, they are often reduced to /ə/ (schwa), which is a relaxed "uh" sound. Notice the stressed and unstressed syllable in each of these words:

🎧 **2.37**   a – **ware**   com – **plete**   suc – **ceed**

The unstressed syllable in all three words has the same sound. Any vowel can be pronounced with schwa.

M 🎧 2.38 Listen to these words. Which syllable has the "uh" sound? Underline it.

1. a - void
2. oc - cur
3. sup - port
4. prob - lem
5. meth - od
6. sys - stem
7. pro - vide
8. com - pare

N Practice pronouncing the words in exercise M. Focus on using the "uh" sound in the unstressed syllables.

O COMMUNICATE Work with a partner. Ask and answer these questions. Use the words in bold in your questions and answers. Pay attention to the "uh" sound in the unstressed syllables.

   A: *If you have a **problem,** who do you usually ask for help?*

   B: *If I have a **problem**, I usually talk to my sister.*

1. If you have a **problem**, who do you usually ask for help?

2. Do you **compare** prices when you shop? What types of things do you **compare**?

3. When does the next holiday **occur?** Do you get a day off from school?

4. What's a good **system** for learning new words?

P Are you ready for a change? Take the quiz to find out. Choose the answers that best describe you. Then add up the number of letters you chose and read the scoring results.

Are you ready for a change?

1 When your alarm goes off in the morning, what do you do?

   a. Get out of bed and start the day.

   b. Feel unhappy for a little while and then get up.

   c. Turn off the alarm and go back to sleep.

2 When you talk to friends or family about making a change in your life, what do they say?

   a. "That's a great idea! We know you can do it!"

   b. They don't have an opinion.

   c. "Hmm . . . maybe that isn't such a good idea."

3 You might have to move to another country for a year. What is your reaction?

   a. I'm excited! I'm ready to go now!

   b. I'll miss my friends, but I'll find ways to keep in touch with them while I'm away.

   c. I'm sad. I will try to avoid the move.

4 You have a part-time job. Your boss wants to promote you—she wants to give you more money and a lot more responsibility. How do you feel?

   a. I deserve this! I'm going to do a great job.

   b. I accept the new job because I need the money, but I'm worried about the new responsibilities.

   c. I don't accept the job.

5 Think about the last big change in your life. How did you handle it?

   a. It was a very positive experience.

   b. It was kind of difficult at first, but I got used to it after awhile.

   c. I really hated everything about it (or I've never really had a big change).

6 How often do you try something new and different?

   a. Probably once a week. I love taking a chance on something new.

   b. Maybe every couple of months, after I think about it for a long time.

   c. I rarely do anything new and different.

Scoring Results

If you chose mostly "a" answers,	you're probably ready for a change. You like to try new things, and you are comfortable in different situations.
If you chose mostly "b" answers,	you are very practical, so making changes will probably work best for you if you do a lot of research and think carefully about the consequences.
If you chose mostly "c" answers,	you're probably not quite ready for a change. It might be better for you to keep things they way they are for awhile.

Q Work in a small group. Were you surprised by your results? Why, or why not?

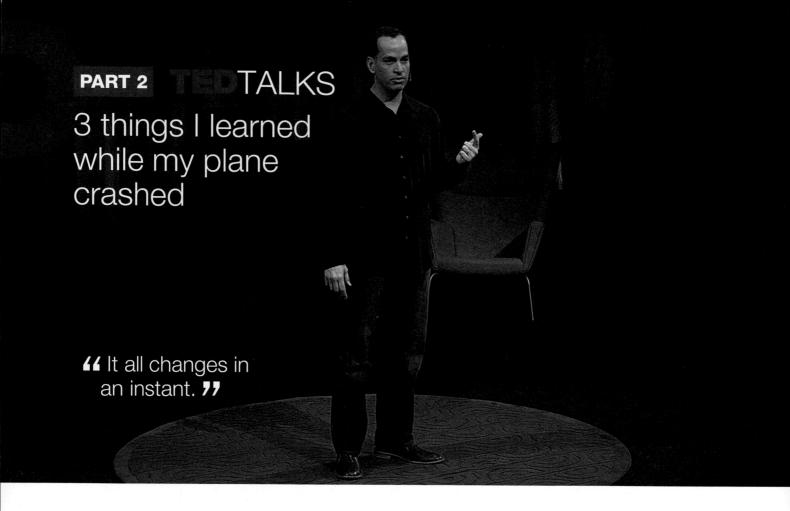

3 things I learned while my plane crashed

" It all changes in an instant. **"**

BEFORE YOU WATCH

A **THINK CRITICALLY Predict.** Read the title and information about the TED speaker. Then answer this question: What do you think this talk will be about? Tell your class.

> **RIC ELIAS** Entrepreneur
>
> Ric Elias was born in Puerto Rico. When he came to the United States to go to college, he didn't know very much English. How did he handle this problem? He says, "(I took only) classes that dealt with numbers my entire first year." He was good at subjects like math and accounting, and taking these classes gave him time to improve his English. Today, Elias runs a successful marketing company. At TED, he talked about an intense experience that changed his life.
>
> Ric Elias's idea worth spreading is that life can change in an instant, so don't delay. Be the best person you can be right now.

B **COMMUNICATE** Work with a partner. Discuss this question:

What motivates people to make big changes in their lives? For example, what types of experiences or life events inspire people to improve themselves?

    A: *I think having children inspires people to improve. What about you?*

    B: *I agree. Another example is getting married.*

VOCABULARY

C 🎧 **2.39** The sentences below will help you learn words in the TED Talk. Read and listen to the sentences. Guess the meaning of each bold word. Then match the sentence parts to make definitions.

a. We are all **unique**; no one is exactly like someone else.

b. There was a loud noise when the plane took off. It gave the passengers a feeling of **terror**.

c. If you want to take a trip, don't **postpone** it. You might not be able to do it later.

d. Some people have a sense of **urgency** about making changes when they realize how short life is.

e. She only had one **regret** in life. She didn't finish college.

f. Because of his **ego**, he was not able to recognize his faults, and he had a difficult time getting along with people at work.

g. I **reflected on** the mistakes I made on the test and then decided to change the way I study.

h. To improve your health, try to **eliminate** bad habits like eating junk food and not getting enough exercise.

i. It looked like the plane was going to crash, but the pilot landed it safely. It was truly a **miracle**.

j. The speaker told the group, "I **challenge** you to try something new and different each day."

1. _____ If you **postpone** something,

2. _____ If you **reflect on** something,

3. _____ A **regret** is

4. _____ If you **challenge** someone to do something,

5. _____ When you **eliminate** something from your life,

6. _____ A person or thing that is **unique** is

7. _____ If you have a feeling of **terror**,

8. _____ A **miracle** is

9. _____ **Ego** refers to

10. _____ **Urgency** is

a. you invite them to do something that takes special effort.

b. the feeling that you need to do something immediately.

c. you remove it permanently.

d. an event that can't be explained by the laws of nature.

e. a bad feeling about something you did in the past.

f. different from the others.

g. a feeling of self-importance.

h. you do it later.

i. you think about it.

j. you feel extreme fear.

D COMMUNICATE Work with a partner. Take turns asking and answering the questions.

> A: *What habit do you want to **eliminate**?*
>
> B: *I want to stop going to sleep so late because I'm always tired in class.*

1. What habit do you want to **eliminate?** Why?

2. What are some things a person should NOT **postpone** in life?

3. In what ways are you **unique**? Think of two things that make you different from other people.

4. What are some activities that require people to **challenge** themselves?

5. What are some things that people often have **regrets** about later in life? Do you have any regrets? What are they?

WATCH

E ▶ 1.39 WATCH FOR MAIN IDEAS As you watch the edited TED Talk, think about Elias's reasons for choosing his topic. Then check [✓] the two reasons that state the main purpose of his talk.

1. _____ to show that something positive can come from a bad experience

2. _____ to explain how birds can cause serious problems for planes

3. _____ to explain some important life lessons

4. _____ to give techniques for surviving a plane crash

5. _____ to explain how to get along better with other people

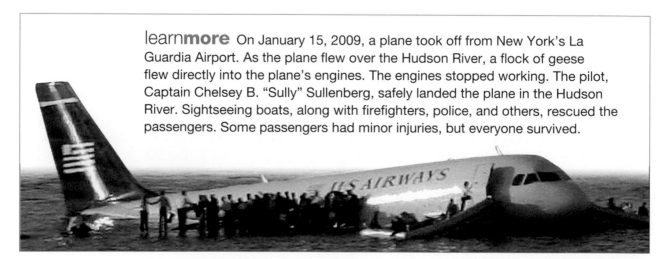

learnmore On January 15, 2009, a plane took off from New York's La Guardia Airport. As the plane flew over the Hudson River, a flock of geese flew directly into the plane's engines. The engines stopped working. The pilot, Captain Chelsey B. "Sully" Sullenberg, safely landed the plane in the Hudson River. Sightseeing boats, along with firefighters, police, and others, rescued the passengers. Some passengers had minor injuries, but everyone survived.

WORDS IN THE TALK
brace for impact (v): get ready to hit something
clear something (v): get over or around; avoid

F THINK CRITICALLY Infer. Work with a partner. Read this excerpt from the talk. Then discuss your answer to the question below.

"And then he [the pilot] says three words. The most unemotional three words I've ever heard. He says, 'Brace for impact.' I didn't have to talk to the flight attendant anymore."

Why didn't Elias have to talk to the flight attendant anymore?

G ▶ 1.40 WATCH FOR DETAILS Watch segment 1 of the edited TED Talk. Then complete the timeline of Elias's flight with the letters of the events in the box.

> **a.** Pilot lines the plane up along the river
>
> **b.** Flight attendants say they hit some birds
>
> **c.** Pilot turns off engines
>
> **d.** There's an explosion
>
> **e.** Pilot turns the plane around

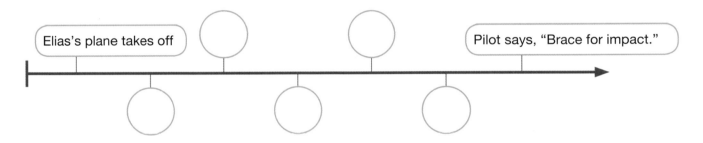

H ▶ 1.41 LISTEN FOR LISTING WORDS Watch segment 2 of the edited TED Talk. Listen for listing words. Number Elias's lessons (1–3) in the order that he presents them.

_____ Dying isn't scary, it's just sad.

_____ Don't waste your time on things that don't matter.

_____ Don't postpone anything.

I ▶ 1.41 WATCH FOR DETAILS Complete the notes on segment 2 of the edited TED Talk. Choose the correct word in parentheses.

Lesson 1

1. Elias realized that things can (*improve / change*) quickly.

2. He thought about all the (*people / relatives*) he wanted to connect with and all the (*fun / experiences*) he wanted to have.

3. This feeling of (*urgency / terror*) changed his life.

Lesson 2

1. Elias (*regretted / remembered*) the time he spent (*doing things / working with people*) that did not matter.

2. He (*regretted / reflected on*) his relationships and decided to (*reduce / eliminate*) negative energy.

3. Today, Elias chooses to be (*right / happy*).

Lesson 3

1. As the plane was coming down, Elias didn't feel (*scared / sad*).

2. He didn't want to leave, though, because he (*loved / missed*) his life.

3. He realized his only (*plan / wish*) was to see his kids grow up.

J ▶ **1.42** **WATCH FOR REPHRASING** Watch this excerpt from the TED Talk. Listen for a rephrasing to answer the questions.

1. What is a "bucket list"? _____

2. Does Elias use any words or expressions to introduce this rephrasing? ☐ Yes ☐ No

K ▶ **1.43** **EXPAND YOUR VOCABULARY** Watch the excerpts from the TED Talk. Guess the meanings of the phrases in the box.

> in an instant   to reach out to   to mend fences   connecting (the) dots

L **WATCH MORE** Go to TED.com to watch the full TED talk by Ric Elias.

AFTER YOU WATCH

M **COMMUNICATE** Work with a partner. Discuss your answers to some of the questions that Elias asks at the end of his talk: If you had an experience like Elias's,

1. ". . . how would you change?"

2. "what would you get done that you're waiting to get done because you think you'll be here forever?"

3. "and more than anything, are you being the best parent [or daughter/son/brother/ sister/friend] you can?"

N **THINK CRITICALLY Interpret an Infographic.** In a survey taken in the U.S., men and women answered the question: *What's on your bucket list?* Work with a partner. Answer these questions about the infographic.

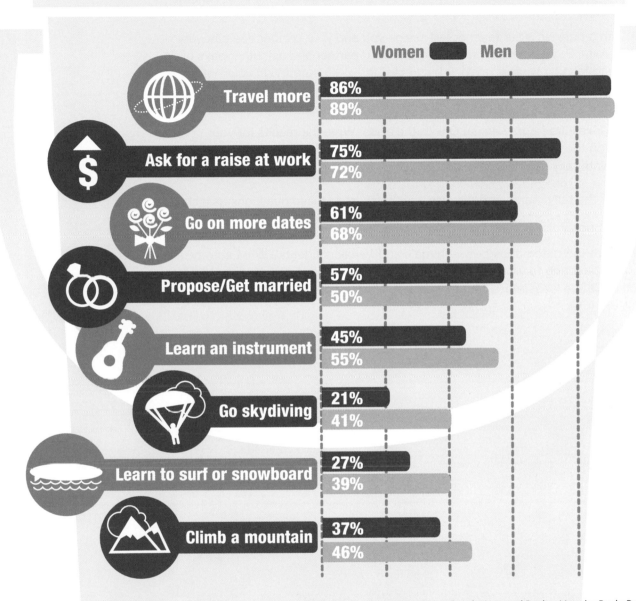

Women ▬ Men ▬

	Women	Men
Travel more	86%	89%
Ask for a raise at work	75%	72%
Go on more dates	61%	68%
Propose/Get married	57%	50%
Learn an instrument	45%	55%
Go skydiving	21%	41%
Learn to surf or snowboard	27%	39%
Climb a mountain	37%	46%

Source: Gallery Creative Group: New Years Resolutions and Bucket Lists, by Paolo Penala

1. What is the most common desire for both men and women?

2. What activity is the least interesting to women?

3. What activity do 46 percent of the men want to do?

4. What activity do 57 percent of the women want to do?

5. Which gender is more interested in getting a raise at work?

O Work with a partner. Compare your answers to the questions in exercise N. Then discuss this question: Did any of the information in the infographic surprise you? Explain your answer.

P As a class, brainstorm some bucket list categories, for example, places to visit, foods to try, sports/activities to try, and so on. Write the categories on the board.

Q Work with a partner. Your teacher will assign you and your partner one category from exercise P. Walk around the room with your partner and ask other pairs of students to tell you what is on their bucket list for your category. In your notebook, take notes on their answers.

R Share your results from exercise Q with the class. Write the results for your category on the board. If more than one student mentioned the same bucket list activity, write tally marks next to it (|||||).

Add up all the tally marks and discuss your answers to these questions as a class:

1. Which bucket list activities are the most popular?

2. What are the differences between male and female students? What activity is the most interesting to women? What activity is the most interesting to men? What activity is the least interesting to women? What activity is the least interesting to men?

A skydiver flying over Ireland

Put It Together

A THINK CRITICALLY Synthesize. Work in a small group. Discuss these questions. Think about the lecture in Part 1 and the edited TED Talk as you discuss.

1. What's the difference between the way the professor describes making changes and the way Elias made changes?

2. Do you think Elias will have to reinforce his new behaviors? Why, or why not?

B THINK CRITICALLY Personalize. Think of examples of how the ideas from the lecture and from the edited TED Talk apply to your own life. Write down a few examples in your notebook.

COMMUNICATE

ASSIGNMENT: Give an Individual Presentation You will give an individual presentation about a change you made or that you want to make. It can be a habit or a behavior, a change in attitude or perspective, or a big life change, such as moving. Review the ideas in Parts 1 and 2 and the listening and speaking skills as you prepare your presentation.

PREPARE

PRESENTATION SKILL Have a Strong Conclusion

You learned that a hook can get the audience's attention. A strong conclusion has the same effect. A strong conclusion focuses the audience on your main idea and gives the audience something to think about after the presentation is over.

To have a strong conclusion, restate your main points and then add a **conclusion device** such as:

- questions
- a call to action
- a quote

Here are some examples of conclusion devices:

Questions: "Are you being the best parent you can?"

A call to action: "So the next time you want to make a change in your life, follow one of my simple rules."

Quote: "As Mahatma Gandhi said, 'You must be the change you wish to see in the world.'"

C Think about a change in your life. First, complete the presentation outline. Include an idea for a conclusion device. Then discuss your outline with a partner. Decide if your partner has a good idea for a strong conclusion.

I. Introduction

    A. Hook idea: _____

    B. Main idea (What did you change?/What do you want to change? Why?):

    _____

    _____

II. Making the Change

    A. Preparation (How did you/will you prepare for the change?):

    _____

    _____

    _____

    B. Process (What steps did you/will you follow? What principles did you/will you use?)

    _____

    _____

    _____

    C. The Challenges (What challenges did you/might you face when making this change?):

    _____

    _____

    _____

III. Conclusion

    A. Restate main idea: _____

    _____

    B. Conclusion device: _____

    _____

D **COLLABORATE** Work with a partner. Practice your presentation. Use your outline from exercise C. As you practice:

- Use listing words and phrases to organize and list your main points.
- Rephrase any words or ideas that your audience might not know.
- Remember to pronounce unstressed vowels with the "uh" sound.

E Read the rubric on page 183 before you present. Notice how your presentation will be evaluated. Keep these categories in mind as you present and watch your classmates' presentations.

PRESENT

F Give your presentation to a small group. Watch your classmates' presentations. After you watch each one, provide feedback using the rubric as a guide. Add notes and any other feedback you want to share.

G **THINK CRITICALLY** Evaluate. In your group, discuss the feedback you received. Discuss what you did well and what might make your presentation stronger.

REFLECT

Reflect on what you have learned. Check [✓] your progress.

I can
- [ ] record definitions.
- [ ] listen for listing words and phrases.
- [ ] rephrase key ideas.
- [ ] pronounce unstressed vowels with the "uh" sound.
- [ ] have a strong conclusion in a presentation.

I understand the meanings of these words and can use them.
Circle those you know. Underline those you need to work more on.

accomplish	desire	factor AWL	punishment	reward
avoid	ego	miracle	reflect on	terror
behavior	eliminate AWL	postpone	regret	unique AWL
challenge AWL	expert AWL	principle AWL	reinforce AWL	urgency

Independent Student Handbook

The *Independent Student Handbook* is a resource you can use during and after this course. It provides additional support for listening, speaking, note-taking, pronunciation, presentation, and vocabulary skills.

Listening Strategies

Predicting

Speakers giving formal talks usually begin by introducing themselves and then introducing their topic. Listen carefully to the introduction of the topic, and try to anticipate what you will hear.

Strategies:

- Use visual information including titles on the board, on slides, or in a PowerPoint presentation.
- Think about what you already know about the topic.
- Ask yourself questions that you think the speaker might answer.
- Listen for specific introduction phrases.

Listening for Main Ideas

It is important to be able to tell the difference between a speaker's main ideas and supporting details. In college, professors will often test students' understanding of the main ideas more than of specific details.

Strategies:

- Listen carefully to the introduction. The main idea is often stated at the end of the introduction.
- Listen for rhetorical questions, or questions that the speaker asks and then answers. Often the answer is the statement of the main idea.
- Notice ideas that are repeated or rephrased. Repetition and rephrasing often signal main ideas (see Common Phrases for Presenting, Repeating and Rephrasing, page 166).

Listening for Details (Examples)

A speaker will often provide examples that support a main idea. A good example can help you understand and remember the main idea better.

Strategies:

- Listen for specific phrases that introduce an example (see Common Phrases for Presenting, Giving Examples, page 166).
- Notice if an example comes after a general statement from the speaker or is leading into a general statement.
- If there are several examples, decide if they all support the same idea.

Listening for Details (Reasons)

Speakers often give reasons or list causes and/or effects to support their ideas.

Strategies:

- Notice nouns that might signal causes/reasons (e.g., *factors, influences, causes, reasons*) or effects/results (e.g., *effects, results, outcomes, consequences*).
- Notice verbs that might signal causes/reasons (e.g., *contribute to, affect, influence, determine, produce, result in*) or effects/results (often these are passive, e.g., *is affected by*).
- Listen for specific phrases that introduce reasons/causes and effects/results (see Common Phrases for Presenting, Giving Reasons or Causes, page 165).

Understanding the Structure of the Presentation

An organized speaker will use certain expressions to alert you to the important information that will follow. Notice signal words and phrases that tell you how the presentation is organized and the relationship between main ideas.

Introduction

A good introduction includes something like a thesis statement, which identifies the topic and gives an idea of how the lecture or presentation will be organized. Here are some expressions to listen for that indicate a speaker is introducing a topic (see also Common Phrases for Presenting, Introducing a Topic, page 165):

I'll be talking about …

My topic is …

There are basically two groups …

There are three reasons …

Body

In the body of the lecture, the speaker will usually expand upon the topic. The speaker will use phrases that tell you the order of events or subtopics and their relationship to each other. Here are some expressions to listen for to help follow the body of a lecture (see also Common Phrases for Presenting, Listing or Sequencing, page 165):

The first / next / final (point) is …

First / Next / Finally, let's look at …

Another reason is …

However, …

Conclusion

In a conclusion, the speaker often summarizes what has already been said and may discuss what it means or make predictions or suggestions. Sometimes speakers ask a question in the conclusion to get the audience to think more about the topic. Here are some expressions to listen for that indicate a speaker is giving a conclusion (see also Common Phrases for Presenting, Conclusion, page 166):

In conclusion, …

In summary, …

As you can see …

To review, + (restatement of main points)

Understanding Meaning from Context

Speakers may use words that are new to you, or you may not understand exactly what they've said. In these situations, you can guess the meaning of a particular word or fill in the gaps of what you've understood by using the context or situation itself.

Strategies:

- Don't panic. You don't always understand every word of what a speaker says in your first language, either.
- Use context clues to fill in the blanks. What did you understand just before or just after the missing part? What did the speaker probably say?
- Listen for words and phrases that signal a definition or explanation (see Common Phrases for Presenting, Signaling a Definition, page 166).

Recognizing a Speaker's Bias

Speakers often have an opinion about the topic they are discussing. It's important for you to know if they are objective or subjective about the topic. Objective speakers do not express an opinion. Subjective speakers have a bias or strong feeling about the topic.

Strategies:

- Notice words like adjectives, adverbs, and modals that the speaker uses (e.g., *ideal, horribly, should, shouldn't*). These suggest that the speaker has a bias.
- Listen to the speaker's tone. Does he or she sound excited, happy, or bored?
- When presenting another point of view on the topic, is that other point of view given much less time and attention by the speaker?
- Listen for words that signal opinions (see Common Phrases for Classroom Communication, Expressing Opinions, page 167).

Common Phrases for Presenting

The chart below provides some common signposts and signal words and phrases that speakers use in the introduction, body, and conclusion of a presentation.

INTRODUCTION

Introducing a Topic

I'm going to talk about …

My topic is …

I'm going to present …

I plan to discuss …

Let's start with …

Today we're going to talk about …

So we're going to show you …

Now/Right/So/Well, (pause) let's look at …

There are three groups/reasons/effects/factors …

There are four steps in this process.

BODY

Listing or Sequencing

First/First of all/The first (noun)/To start/To begin, …

Second/Secondly/The second/Next/Another/Also/Then/In addition, …

Last/The last/Finally …

There are many/several/three types/kinds of/ways, …

Signaling Problems/Solutions

The one problem/issue/challenge (with) is …

The one solution/answer/response is …

Giving Reasons or Causes

Because + (clause): Because it makes me feel happy …

Because of + (noun phrase): Because of climate change …

Due to + (noun phrase) …

Since + (clause) …

The reason that I like hip-hop is …

One reason that people listen to music is …

One factor is + (noun phrase) …

The main reason that…

Giving Results or Effects

so + (clause): so I went to the symphony

Therefore, + (sentence): Therefore, I went to the symphony.

As a result, + (sentence).

Consequently, + (sentence).

… causes + (noun phrase)

… leads to + (noun phrase)

… had an impact/effect on + (noun phrase)

If … then …

Giving Examples

The first example is…

Here's an example of what I mean …

For instance, …

For example, …

Let me give you an example …

… such as …

… like …

Repeating and Rephrasing

What you need to know is …

I'll say this again, …

So again, let me repeat …

The most important point is …

Signaling Additional Examples or Ideas

Not only … but, besides

Besides …

Not only do … but also

Signaling to Stop Taking Notes

You don't need this for the test.

This information is in your books / on your handout / on the website.

You don't have to write all this down.

Identifying a Side Track

This is off-topic, …

On a different subject, …

As an aside, …

That reminds me ….

Returning to a Previous Topic

Getting back to our previous discussion, …

To return to our earlier topic …

OK, getting back on topic …

So to return to what we were saying, …

Signaling a Definition

Which means …

What that means is …

Or …

In other words, …

Another way to say that is …

That is …

That is to say …

Talking about Visuals

This graph / infographic / diagram shows / explains …

The line / box image represents …

The main point of this visual is …

You can see …

From this we can see …

CONCLUSION

Concluding

Well / So, that's how I see it.

In conclusion, …

In summary, …

To sum up, …

As you can see, …

At the end, …

To review, + (restatement of main points)

Common Phrases For Classroom Communication

The chart below shows some common phrases for expressing ideas and opinions in class and for interacting with your classmates during pair and group work exercises.

PHRASES FOR EXPRESSING YOURSELF

Expressing Opinions	Expressing Likes and Dislikes
I think …	*I like …*
I believe …	*I prefer …*
I'm sure …	*I love …*
In my opinion/view …	*I can't stand …*
If you ask me, …	*I hate …*
Personally, …	*I really don't like …*
To me, …	*I don't care for …*

Giving Facts	Giving Tips or Suggestions
There is evidence/proof …	Imperatives (e.g., *Try to get more sleep.*)
Experts claim/argue …	*You/We should/shouldn't …*
Studies show …	*You/We ought to …*
Researchers found …	*It's (not) a good idea to …*
The record shows …	*I suggest (that) …*
	Let's …
	How about + (noun/gerund)
	What about + (noun/gerund)
	Why don't we/you …
	You/We could …

PHRASES FOR INTERACTING WITH OTHERS

Agreeing	Clarifying/Checking Your Understanding
I agree.	*So are you saying that … ?*
True.	*So what you mean is … ?*
Good point.	*What do you mean?*
Exactly.	*How's that?*
Absolutely.	*How so?*
I was just about to say that.	*I'm not sure I understand/follow.*
Definitely.	*Do you mean … ?*
Right!	*I'm not sure what you mean.*

PHRASES FOR INTERACTING WITH OTHERS

Disagreeing

I disagree.

I'm not so sure about that.

I don't know.

That's a good point, but I don't agree.

I see what you mean, but I think that …

Checking Others' Understanding

Does that make sense?

Do you understand?

Do you see what I mean?

Is that clear?

Are you following me?

Do you have any questions?

Asking for Opinions

What do you think?

We haven't heard from you in a while.

Do you have anything to add?

What are your thoughts?

How do you feel?

What's your opinion?

Taking Turns

Can I say something?

May I say something?

Could I add something?

Can I just say … ?

May I continue?

Can I finish what I was saying?

Would you finish what you were saying?

Did you finish your thought?

Let me finish.

Let's get back to …

Interrupting Politely

Excuse me.

Pardon me.

Forgive me for interrupting, …

I hate to interrupt, but …

Can I stop you for a second?

Asking for Repetition

Could you say that again?

I'm sorry?

I didn't catch what you said.

I'm sorry. I missed that. What did you say?

Could you repeat that, please?

Showing Interest

I see.

Good for you.

Really?

Seriously?

Um-hmm.

No kidding!

Wow.

And? (Then what?)

That's funny / amazing / incredible / awful!

Note-Taking Strategies

Taking notes is a personalized skill. It is important to develop a note-taking system that works well for you. However, there are some common strategies that you can use to improve your note-taking.

BEFORE YOU LISTEN

Focus Try to clear your mind before the speaker begins so you can pay attention. If possible, review previous notes or what you already know about the topic.

Predict If you know the topic of the talk, think about what you might hear.

LISTEN

Take Notes by Hand

Research suggests that taking notes by hand rather than on a laptop or tablet is more effective. Taking notes by hand requires you to summarize, rephrase, and synthesize the information. This helps you *encode* the information, or put it into a form that you can understand and remember.

Listen for Signal Words and Phrases

Speakers often use signal words and phrases (see page 168) to organize their ideas and indicate what they are going to talk about. Listening for signal words and phrases can help you decide what information to write down in your notes.

Today we're going to talk about three alternative methods that are ecofriendly, fast, and efficient.

Condense (Shorten) Information

- As you listen, focus on the most important ideas. The speaker will usually repeat, define, explain, and/or give examples of these ideas. Take notes on these ideas.

    Speaker: *Worldwide, people are using and wasting huge amounts of plastic. For example, Americans throw away 35 million plastic bottles a year.*

    Notes: *Waste plastic*
    Amer. 35 mil plastic bottles/year

- Don't write full sentences. Write only key words (nouns, verbs, adjectives), phrases, or short sentences.

    Full sentence: *The Maldives built a sea wall around the main island of Male.*

    Notes: *Built sea wall—Male*

- Leave out information that is obvious.

    Full sentence: *Van den Bercken fell in love with the music of Handel.*

    Notes: *VBD loves Handel*

- Write numbers and statistics. (*35 mil; 91%*)
- Use abbreviations (e.g., ft., min., yr) and symbols (=, ≠, >, <, %, →)
- Use indenting. Write main ideas on left side of paper. Indent details.

    Benefits of car sharing

    Save $

    Saved $300-400/mo.

- Write details under key terms to help you remember them.

• Write the definitions of important new words from the presentation.

AFTER YOU LISTEN

• Review your notes soon after the lecture or presentation. Add any details you missed and remember.
• Clarify anything you don't understand in your notes with a classmate or teacher.
• Add or highlight main ideas. Cross out details that aren't important or necessary.
• Rewrite anything that is hard to read or understand. Rewrite your notes in an outline or other graphic organizer to organize the information more clearly (see Organizing Information, below).
• Use arrows, boxes, diagrams, or other visual cues to show relationships between ideas.

ORGANIZING INFORMATION

Sometimes it is helpful to take notes using a graphic organizer. You can use one to take notes while you are listening or to organize your notes after you listen. Here are some examples of graphic organizers:

Flowcharts are used to show processes, or cause/effect relationships.

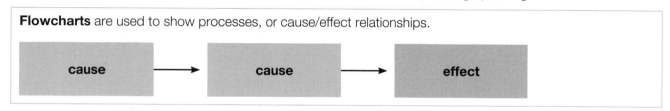

Mind maps show the connection between concepts. The main idea is usually in the center with supporting ideas and details around it.

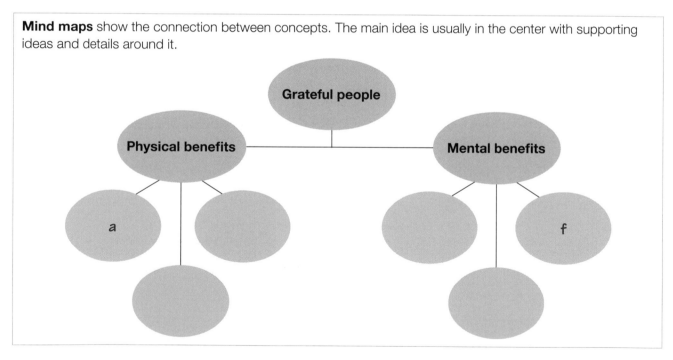

Outlines show the relationship between main ideas and details.

To use an outline for taking notes, write the main ideas starting at the left margin of your paper. Below the main ideas, indent and write the supporting ideas and details. You may do this as you listen, or go back and rewrite your notes as an outline later.

    I. Saving Water

        A. Why is it crucial to save water?

            1. Save money

            2. Not enough fresh water in the world

T-charts compare two topics.

Hands-On Learning	
Advantages	**Disadvantages**
1. Uses all the senses (sight, touch, etc.)	1. Requires many types of materials
2. Encourages student participation	2. May be more difficult to manage large classes
3. Helps memory	3. Requires more teacher time to prepare

Timelines show a sequence of events.

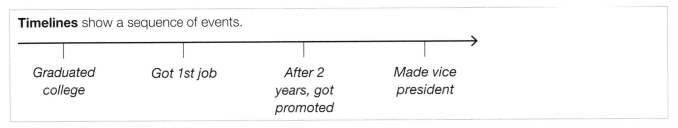

| Graduated college | Got 1st job | After 2 years, got promoted | Made vice president |

Venn diagrams compare and contrast two or more topics. The overlapping areas show similarities.

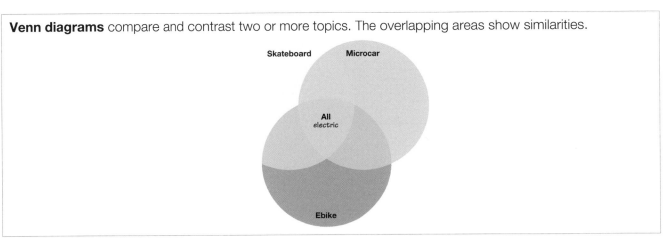

Pronunciation Strategies

When speaking English, it's important to pay attention to the pronunciation of specific sounds. It is also important to learn how to use rhythm, stress, and pausing. The charts below provide some tips about English pronunciation.

SPECIFIC SOUNDS

Vowels			Consonants		
Symbol	Key Word	Pronunciation	Symbol	Key Word	Pronunciation
/ɑ/	hot	/hɑt/	/b/	boy	/bɔɪ/
	far	/fɑr/	/d/	day	/deɪ/
/æ/	cat	/kæt/	/ʤ/	just	/ʤʌst/
/aɪ/	fine	/faɪn/	/f/	face	/feɪs/
/aʊ/	house	/haʊs/	/g/	get	/gɛt/
/ɛ/	bed	/bɛd/	/h/	hat	/hæt/
/eɪ/	name	/neɪm/	/k/	car	/kɑr/
/i/	need	/nid/	/l/	light	/laɪt/
/ɪ/	sit	/sɪt/	/m/	my	/maɪ/
/oʊ/	go	/goʊ/	/n/	nine	/naɪn/
/ʊ/	book	/bʊk/	/ŋ/	sing	/sɪŋ/
/u/	boot	/but/	/p/	pen	/pɛn/
/ɔ/	dog	/dɔg/	/r/	right	/raɪt/
	four	/fɔr/	/s/	see	/si/
/ɔɪ/	toy	/tɔɪ/	/t/	tea	/ti/
/ʌ/	cup	/kʌp/	/ʧ/	cheap	/ʧip/
/ɛr/	bird	/bɛrd/	/v/	vote	/voʊt/
/ə/	about	/ə'baʊt/	/w/	west	/wɛst/
	after	/'æftər/	/y/	yes	/yɛs/
			/z/	zoo	/zu/
			/ð/	they	/ðeɪ/
			/θ/	think	/θɪŋk/
			/ʃ/	shoe	/ʃu/
			/ʒ/	vision	/'vɪʒən/

Source: *The Newbury House Dictionary plus Grammar Reference*, Fifth Edition, National Geographic Learning/ Cengage Learning, 2014.

RHYTHM

The rhythm of English involves stress and pausing.

Stress

- English words are based on syllables—units of sound that include one vowel sound.
- In every word in English, one syllable has the strongest stress.
- In English, speakers group words that go together based on the meaning and context of the sentence. These groups of words are called *thought groups*. In each thought group, one word is stressed more than the others—the stress is placed on the stressed syllable in this word.
- In general, new ideas and information are stressed.

Pausing

- Pauses in English can be divided into two groups: long and short pauses.
- English speakers use long pauses to mark the conclusion of a thought, items in a list, or choices given.
- Short pauses are used between thought groups to break up the ideas in sentences into smaller, more manageable chunks of information.

INTONATION

English speakers use intonation, or pitch (the rise and fall of their voice), to help express meaning. For example, speakers usually use a rising intonation at the end of *yes/no* questions, and a falling intonation at the end of *wh-* questions and statements.

Presentaton Strategies

You will often have to give individual or group presentations in your class. The strategies below will help you to prepare, present, and reflect on your presentations.

PREPARE

As you prepare your presentation:

Consider Your Topic

- *Choose a topic you feel passionate about.* If you are passionate about your topic, your audience will be more interested and excited about your topic, too. Focus on one major idea that you can bring to life. The best ideas are the ones your audience wants to experience.

Consider Your Purpose

- *Have a strong beginning.* Use an effective *hook*, such as a quote, an interesting example, a rhetorical question, or a powerful image to get your audience's attention. Include one sentence that explains what you will do in your presentation and why.
- *Stay focused.* Make sure your details and examples support your main points. Avoid sidetracks or unnecessary information that takes you away from your topic.
- *Use visuals that relate to your ideas.* Drawings, photos, video clips, infographics, charts, maps, slides, and physical objects can get your audience's attention and explain ideas effectively, quickly, and clearly. For example, a photo or map of a location you mention can help your audience picture a place they have never been. Slides with only key words and phrases can help emphasize your main points. Visuals should be bright, clear, and simple.

- *Have a strong conclusion.* A strong conclusion should serve the same purpose as the strong beginning—to get your audience's attention and make them think. Good conclusions often refer back to the introduction, or beginning, of the presentation. For example, if you ask a question in the beginning, you can answer it in the conclusion. Remember to restate your main points, and add a conclusion device such as a question, a call to action, or a quote.

Consider Your Audience

- *Share a personal story.* You can also present information that will get an emotional reaction; for example, information that will make your audience feel surprised, curious, worried, or upset. This will help your audience relate to you and your topic.

- *Use familiar concepts.* Think about the people in your audience. Ask yourself these questions: Where are they from? How old are they? What is their background? What do they already know about my topic? What information do I need to explain? Use language and concepts they will understand.

- *Be authentic (be yourself!).* Write your presentation yourself. Use words that you know and are comfortable using.

Rehearse

- *Make an outline* to help you organize your ideas.

- *Write notes on notecards.* Do not write full sentences, just key words and phrases to help you remember important ideas. Mark the words you should stress and places to pause.

- *Review the pronunciation skills* in your book. Check the pronunciation of words you are uncertain about with a classmate, a teacher, or in a dictionary. Note and practice the pronunciation of difficult words.

- *Memorize the introduction and conclusion.* Rehearse your presentation several times. Practice saying it out loud to yourself (perhaps in front of a mirror or video recorder) and in front of others.

- *Ask for feedback.* Note and revise material that doesn't flow smoothly based on feedback and on your own performance in rehearsal. If specific words or phrases are still a problem, rephrase them.

PRESENT

As you present:

- Pay attention to your pacing (how fast or slow you speak). Remember to speak slowly and clearly. Pause to allow your audience to process information.

- Speak at a volume loud enough to be heard by everyone in the audience, but not too loud. Ask the audience if your volume is OK at the beginning of your talk.

- Vary your intonation. Don't speak in the same tone throughout the talk. Your audience will be more interested if your voice rises and falls, speeds up and slows down to match the ideas you are talking about.

- Be friendly and relaxed with your audience. Remember to smile!

- Show enthusiasm for your topic. Use humor if appropriate.

- Have a relaxed body posture. Don't stand with your arms folded or look down at your notes. Use gestures when helpful to emphasize your points.

- Don't read directly from your notes. Use them to help you remember ideas.

- Don't look at or read from your visuals too much. Use them to support and illustrate your ideas.

- Use frequent eye contact with the entire audience.

REFLECT

As you reflect on your presentation:

- *Consider what you think went well* during your presentation and what areas you can improve upon.

- *Get feedback* from your classmates and teacher. How do their comments relate to your own thoughts about your presentation? Did they notice things you didn't? How can you use their feedback in your next presentation?

Vocabulary Learning Strategies

Vocabulary learning is an on-going process. The strategies below will help you learn and remember new vocabulary words.

Guessing Meaning from Context

You can often guess the meaning of an unfamiliar word by looking at or listening to the words and sentences around it. Speakers usually know when a word is unfamiliar to the audience, or is essential to understanding the main ideas, and will often provide clues as to its meaning.

- Restatement or synonym: A speaker may give a synonym to explain the meaning of a word, using phrases such as, *in other words, also called, or …, also known as*.

- Antonyms: A speaker may define a word by explaining what it is NOT. The speaker might say *Unlike A / In contrast to A, B is …*

- Definition: Listen for signals such as *which means* or *is defined as*. Definitions can also be signaled by a pause.

- Examples: A speaker may provide examples that can help you figure out what something is. For example, *Paris-Plage is a **recreation** area on the River Seine, in Paris, France. It has a sandy beach, a swimming pool, and areas for inline skating, playing volleyball, and other activities.*

Understanding Word Families: Stems, Prefixes, and Suffixes

Use your understanding of stems, prefixes, and suffixes to recognize unfamiliar words and to expand your vocabulary. A stem is the root part of the word, which provides the main meaning.

A prefix is before the stem and usually modifies meaning (e.g., adding *re-* to a word means "again"). A suffix is after the stem and usually changes the part of speech (e.g., adding *–ation / –sion / –ion* to a verb changes it to a noun). For example, in the word *endangered*, the stem or root is *danger*, the prefix is *en–*, and the suffix is *–ed*. Words that share the same stem or root belong to the same word family (e.g., *event, eventful, uneventful, uneventfully*).

Word Stem	Meaning	Example
ann (or enn)	year	anniversary, millennium
chron(o)	time	chronological, synchronize
flex (or flect)	bend	flexible, reflection
graph	draw, write	graphics, paragraph
lab	work	labor, collaborate
mob	move	mobility, automobile
sect	cut	sector, bisect
vac	empty	vacant, evacuate

Prefix	Meaning	Example
auto-	self	automatic, autonomy
bi-	two	bilingual, bicycle
dis-	not, negation, remove	disappear, disadvantages
inter-	between	Internet, international
mis-	bad, badly, incorrectly	misunderstand, misjudge
pre-	before	prehistoric, preheat
re-	again; back	repeat; return
trans-	across, beyond	transfer, translate

Suffix	Part of Speech	Example
-able (or *-ible*)	adjective	believable, impossible
-en	verb	lengthen, strengthen
-ful	adjective	beautiful, successful
-ize	verb	modernize, summarize
-ly	adverb; adjective	carefully, happily; friendly, lonely
-ment	noun	assignment, statement
-tion (or *-sion*)	noun	education, occasion
-wards	adverb	backwards, forwards

Using a Dictionary

A dictionary is a useful tool to help you understand unfamiliar vocabulary you read or hear. Here are some helpful tips for using a dictionary:

- When you see or hear a new word, try to guess its part of speech (noun, verb, adjective, etc.) and meaning, then look it up in a dictionary.

- Some words have multiple meanings. Look up a new word in the dictionary, and try choose the correct meaning for the context. Then see if it makes sense within the context.

- When you look up a word, look at all the definitions to see if there is a basic core meaning. This will help you understand the word when it is used in a different context. Also look at all the related words, or words in the same family. This can help you expand your vocabulary. For example, the core meaning of *structure* involves something built or put together.

struc·ture /ˈstrʌktʃər/ *n.* **1** [C] a building of any kind: *A new structure is being built on the corner.* **2** [C] any architectural object of any kind: *The Eiffel Tower is a famous Parisian structure.* **3** [U] the way parts are put together or organized: *the structure of a song‖a business's structure*
—*v.* [T] **-tured, -turing, -tures** to put together or organize parts of s.t.: *We are structuring a plan to hire new teachers.* *-adj.* **structural.**

Source: *The Newbury House Dictionary plus Grammar Reference*, Fifth Edition, National Geographic Learning/ Cengage Learning, 2014.

Multi-Word Units

You can improve your fluency if you learn and use vocabulary as multi-word units: idioms (*mend fences*), collocations (*trial and error*), and fixed expressions (*in other words*). Some multi-word units can only be understood as a chunk—the individual words do not add up to the same overall meaning. Keep track of multi-word units in a notebook or on notecards.

Vocabulary Note Cards

You can expand your vocabulary by using vocabulary note cards. Write the word, expression, or sentence that you want to learn on one side. On the other, draw a four-square grid and write the following information in the squares: definition; translation (in your first language); sample sentence; synonyms. Choose words that are high frequency or on the academic word list. If you have looked a word up a few times, you should make a card for it.

definition:	*first language translation:*
sample sentence:	*synonyms:*

Organize the cards in review sets so you can practice them. Don't put words that are similar in spelling or meaning in the same review set, as you may get them mixed up. Go through the cards and test yourself on the meanings of the words or expressions. You can also practice with a partner.

TED Talk Summary Worksheet

Unit: _____   Video Title: _____

Speaker: _____

What information did you learn about the speaker and his or her background?

_____

_____

_____

What hook does the speaker use?

_____

Summarize the main idea in one sentence.

_____

What was the most interesting part of the Talk? What would you tell a friend about it?

_____

_____

_____

How does the speaker engage the audience? (e.g., photos, infographics, other visuals, humor, gestures, personal story)

_____

How does the speaker conclude the talk? (e.g., call to action, question)

_____

What is your opinion of the talk? What words would you use to describe it?

_____

_____

What words or phrases in the talk are new to you? Write three and their definitions.

_____

_____

_____

Copyright © 2017 National Geographic Learning, a part of Cengage Learning. Permission granted to photocopy for use in class.

Presentation Scoring Rubrics

Unit 1

Note: 1= lowest; 5 = highest

The presenter ...

Name _____ Name _____ Name _____ Name _____

The presenter ...	Name					Name					Name					Name				
1. was clear and organized.	1	2	3	4	5	1	2	3	4	5	1	2	3	4	5	1	2	3	4	5
2. focused on one topic.	1	2	3	4	5	1	2	3	4	5	1	2	3	4	5	1	2	3	4	5
3. stated the resource and gave examples of how we use it.	1	2	3	4	5	1	2	3	4	5	1	2	3	4	5	1	2	3	4	5
4. used the imperative, *should/shouldn't*, or *it's (not) a good idea* to give tips.	1	2	3	4	5	1	2	3	4	5	1	2	3	4	5	1	2	3	4	5
5. used correct syllable stress.	1	2	3	4	5	1	2	3	4	5	1	2	3	4	5	1	2	3	4	5
Overall Rating	1	2	3	4	5	1	2	3	4	5	1	2	3	4	5	1	2	3	4	5
What did you like?																				
What could be improved?																				

Unit 2

Note: 1= lowest; 5 = highest

The presenter ...

Name _____ Name _____ Name _____ Name _____

The presenter ...	Name					Name					Name					Name				
1. was clear and organized.	1	2	3	4	5	1	2	3	4	5	1	2	3	4	5	1	2	3	4	5
2. used descriptive language.	1	2	3	4	5	1	2	3	4	5	1	2	3	4	5	1	2	3	4	5
3. used a visual aid effectively.	1	2	3	4	5	1	2	3	4	5	1	2	3	4	5	1	2	3	4	5
4. divided long sentences into thought groups and paused appropriately.	1	2	3	4	5	1	2	3	4	5	1	2	3	4	5	1	2	3	4	5
Overall Rating	1	2	3	4	5	1	2	3	4	5	1	2	3	4	5	1	2	3	4	5
What did you like?																				
What could be improved?																				

Unit 3

Note: 1= lowest; 5 = highest

The presenter …	Name _____					Name _____					Name _____					Name _____				
1. was clear and organized.	1	2	3	4	5	1	2	3	4	5	1	2	3	4	5	1	2	3	4	5
2. used listing signals.	1	2	3	4	5	1	2	3	4	5	1	2	3	4	5	1	2	3	4	5
3. used correct statement intonation.	1	2	3	4	5	1	2	3	4	5	1	2	3	4	5	1	2	3	4	5
4. had clearly rehearsed before presenting.	1	2	3	4	5	1	2	3	4	5	1	2	3	4	5	1	2	3	4	5
Overall Rating	1	2	3	4	5	1	2	3	4	5	1	2	3	4	5	1	2	3	4	5
What did you like?																				
What could be improved?																				

Unit 4

Note: 1= lowest; 5 = highest

The presenter …	Name _____					Name _____					Name _____					Name _____				
1. was clear and organized.	1	2	3	4	5	1	2	3	4	5	1	2	3	4	5	1	2	3	4	5
2. used an effective hook.	1	2	3	4	5	1	2	3	4	5	1	2	3	4	5	1	2	3	4	5
3. used words and expressions to give reasons.	1	2	3	4	5	1	2	3	4	5	1	2	3	4	5	1	2	3	4	5
4. pronounced contractions with *be* correctly.	1	2	3	4	5	1	2	3	4	5	1	2	3	4	5	1	2	3	4	5
Overall Rating	1	2	3	4	5	1	2	3	4	5	1	2	3	4	5	1	2	3	4	5
What did you like?																				
What could be improved?																				

Unit 5

Note: 1= lowest; 5 = highest

The presenter ...	Name _____	Name _____	Name _____	Name _____
1. was clear and organized.	1 2 3 4 5	1 2 3 4 5	1 2 3 4 5	1 2 3 4 5
2. introduced main points with key words and phrases.	1 2 3 4 5	1 2 3 4 5	1 2 3 4 5	1 2 3 4 5
3. told a personal story that was interesting, easy to follow, and supported the message.	1 2 3 4 5	1 2 3 4 5	1 2 3 4 5	1 2 3 4 5
4. used correct sentence stress.	1 2 3 4 5	1 2 3 4 5	1 2 3 4 5	1 2 3 4 5
Overall Rating	1 2 3 4 5	1 2 3 4 5	1 2 3 4 5	1 2 3 4 5
What did you like?				
What could be improved?				

Unit 6

Note: 1= lowest; 5 = highest

The presenter ...	Name _____	Name _____	Name _____	Name _____
1. was clear and organized.	1 2 3 4 5	1 2 3 4 5	1 2 3 4 5	1 2 3 4 5
2. made the presentation appropriate for the audience.	1 2 3 4 5	1 2 3 4 5	1 2 3 4 5	1 2 3 4 5
3. talked about what they were curious about, how they found the answer, and how they felt about it.	1 2 3 4 5	1 2 3 4 5	1 2 3 4 5	1 2 3 4 5
Overall Rating	1 2 3 4 5	1 2 3 4 5	1 2 3 4 5	1 2 3 4 5
What did you like?				
What could be improved?				

Unit 7

Note: 1= lowest; 5 = highest

The presenter …	Name _____	Name _____	Name _____	Name _____
1. was clear and organized.	1 2 3 4 5	1 2 3 4 5	1 2 3 4 5	1 2 3 4 5
2. was organized logically; problems → solutions or solutions → problems.	1 2 3 4 5	1 2 3 4 5	1 2 3 4 5	1 2 3 4 5
3. used words and expressions to talk about problems and solutions.	1 2 3 4 5	1 2 3 4 5	1 2 3 4 5	1 2 3 4 5
4. used linking correctly.	1 2 3 4 5	1 2 3 4 5	1 2 3 4 5	1 2 3 4 5
Overall Rating	1 2 3 4 5	1 2 3 4 5	1 2 3 4 5	1 2 3 4 5
What did you like?				
What could be improved?				

Unit 8

Note: 1= lowest; 5 = highest

The presenter …	Name _____	Name _____	Name _____	Name _____
1. was clear and organized.	1 2 3 4 5	1 2 3 4 5	1 2 3 4 5	1 2 3 4 5
2. used listing words to signal main points.	1 2 3 4 5	1 2 3 4 5	1 2 3 4 5	1 2 3 4 5
3. correctly pronounced unstressed vowels.	1 2 3 4 5	1 2 3 4 5	1 2 3 4 5	1 2 3 4 5
4. used rephrasing, if necessary.	1 2 3 4 5	1 2 3 4 5	1 2 3 4 5	1 2 3 4 5
5. had a strong conclusion.				
Overall Rating	1 2 3 4 5	1 2 3 4 5	1 2 3 4 5	1 2 3 4 5
What did you like?				
What could be improved?				

Vocabulary Index

Credits

Photo Credits

Cover: Andrew Rowat/The Image Bank/Getty Images

2–3 © Arnaud Finistre, **4** Bloomberg/Getty Images, **7** Bartosz Hadyniak/E+/Getty Images, **9** (t) Danny Smythe/Shutterstock.com, (bl) Incorrect Image/Shutterstock.com, **11** Pete Mcbride/National Geographic Creative, **12–13** © TED, **15** Britt Erlanson/Cultura/Getty Images, **16–17** Ueslei Marcelino/Reuters, **22–23** Yanai Bonneh/500px Prime, **24** Frans Lanting/National Geographic Creative, **26** (bl) Beverly Joubert/National Geographic Creative, (br) David Griffin/National Geographic Creative, **27** (tl) Subhrojyoti Banerjee/National Geographic Creative, (tr) Jean Brooks/Robertharding/Getty Images, **31** © Info We Trust/RJ Andrews, **32** © James Duncan Davidson/TED, **33** Carsten Peter/National Geographic Creative, **36** Dan Callister/Alamy Stock Photo, **38** Francis Lavigne-theriault/500px Prime, **42–43** Hemis/Alamy Stock Photo, **44** China Daily/Reuters, **49** Jeff T. Green/Getty Images News/Getty Images, **51** EPA European Pressphoto Agency b.v./Alamy Stock Photo, **52** © James Duncan Davidson/TED, **55** © Boosted Board, **57** ViewStock/Getty Images, **62–63** © Terra Fondriest, **64** © Mirco Balboni, **66** Andy Sheppard/Redferns/Getty Images, **68** © Nikola Smernic, **71** Greg Davis/National Geographic Creative, **72** © James Duncan Davidson/TED, **75** Alfredo Dagli Orti/The Art Archive at Art Resource, NY, **77** © Handel at the Piano, **82–83** Wally Skalij/Los Angeles Times/Getty Images, **84** Stephen Ford/Alamy Stock Photo, **89** Simon Potter/Cultura/Aurora Photos, **90** David Lees/DigitalVision/Getty Images, **92** © TED, **93** Steve Debenport/E+/Getty Images, **96** © TED, **98** Andrea Crisante/Shutterstock.com, **101** Rawpixel Ltd/iStock/Getty Images Plus/Getty Images, **102–103** Peter Terren/Barcroft USA/Getty Images, **104** Sonic/500px Prime, **106** Design Pics Inc/National Geographic Creative, **108** © James Friedman Photography, **112–113** © TED, **115** Paul Nicklen/National Geographic Creative, **117** Mischa Keijser/Cultura/Getty Images, **119** Fuse/Corbis/Getty Images, **122–123** Gardel Bertrand/hemis.fr/Getty Images, **124** Robert Harding/Aurora Photos, **126** © Iwan Baan Photography, **129** Siana Avramova/Alamy Stock Photo, **131** © Ryan Lash/TED, **133** H. Armstrong Roberts/Retrofile/Getty Images, **134** Marc Dozier/Corbis Documentary/Getty Images, **137** Pakhnyushcha/Shutterstock.com, **138** William Albert Allard/National Geographic Creative, **139** © Pim Hendriksen, **142–143** Fairfax Media/Getty Images, **144** Cory Richards/National Geographic Creative, **146** Klaus Vedfelt/DigitalVision/Getty Images, **148** Peter Beavis/The Image Bank/Getty Images, **152** © TED, **154** Brendan McDermid/Reuters, **158** Kevin Elvis King/Moment Select/Getty Images, **162** Brendan McDermid/Reuters.